the girl *on the* bathroom floor

the girl *on the* bathroom floor

HELD TOGETHER WHEN
EVERYTHING IS FALLING APART

Amber Emily Smith

W PUBLISHING GROUP

AN IMPRINT OF THOMAS NELSON

To Granger—
Grateful to walk hand in hand with you through the valleys
and rejoice with you on the mountaintops. I thank God every
day for your love, wisdom, strength, and steadfast leading.
One day closer to eternity.

CONTENTS

CONTENTS

AFTER

LETTER TO THE GIRL
ON THE BATHROOM FLOOR

Blessed be the God and Father of our Lord Jesus Christ,
the Father of mercies and God of all comfort, who comforts
us in all our affliction, so that we may be able to comfort
those who are in any affliction, with the comfort with
which we ourselves are comforted by God. For as we share
abundantly in Christ's sufferings, so through Christ we
share abundantly in comfort too.

2 Corinthians 1:3–5

Hey, you—

Can I come in? I'm Amber and I'd love to sit with you for a few
moments, if that's okay. To simply be here, beside you. With you. I
want to lie down on the tiles next to you and look into your tired,
tear-filled eyes and say, "I see you. I understand. I hate that you are
going through this pain. I know how deeply it hurts, and I am so,
so sorry." I don't want to jump right in and tell you all the ways that

this will get better or how God has a plan for this awful thing you are going through, because I know you don't want to hear that right now. You want your life the way it was. You want your marriage healed, your finances restored, your child to stop abusing drugs. You want the cancer gone; your spouse, your mom, your friend, or even your sweet baby back in your arms; you just want this pain to stop. I know.

There is no pretty path in walking through the disappointments and traumas we face. Sometimes life is just plain hard, and some days it takes all you have just to survive. There is a time to mourn and lament and grieve your losses and pain, and maybe that's where you are right now—at your lowest, in the depths, gasping for even the next breath to keep going. But I know that when I felt like you, I didn't want to stay stuck in that darkness there on the bathroom floor, and I don't want you to either. I need you to know that *you are not alone*. And as much as this hurts, there is hope. It won't always feel like this.

This is a book about the deepest pain I have ever known and the One who carried me through it. It's for you. And for me. It's for those of us whose lives haven't unfolded the way we hoped—for those of us whose dreams have been shattered, for the lonely, for all of us who find ourselves questioning the goodness of God in a world of hurt. For those of us who are in the throes of unexpected, sudden suffering, and for those of us who have been navigating pain for decades.

It's for those of us who find ourselves on the bathroom floor, soaked in our own tears, overwhelmed by the weight of this fallen place, and wondering how we will ever keep going. Maybe you've lost a child, like I have, maybe your marriage is broken, or you've buried your spouse. Maybe you live with chronic pain, or you have found yourself in financial ruin, or you've just received news of a diagnosis you never saw coming, or the cancer is back and it's spreading. Perhaps you are anxious, depressed, exhausted, lonely, or stuck in a cycle of addiction and shame you can't seem to get out of. Maybe you've been betrayed by someone you were closest to. Whatever has brought you to this place, you're not alone.

This is a book about hope, a book about transformation, even in the midst of unimaginable suffering. It's the story about my discovering not just who I was but who God created me to be. It's a story about searching for who God is and where He is in our pain. This is a book about a girl who *was*, about a girl who died when her son died, and about a girl raised to new life in Christ.

If you're in the middle of a battle and don't know how you'll make it, or if you just want to be prepared for when the storms of this life come (because they will), this book is for you. Whether you're just beginning to walk through grief or have been carrying it for years, whether you know Jesus or are searching for answers, you'll find a piece of my heart here and a compass directing you to our Living Hope and the unfailing peace and freedom that only He can give.

This is a story of searching for light in the darkness, of finding hope through suffering, and of being met at my lowest by He who is highest. It's the story of a woman broken by tragedy and rebuilt by the goodness and grace of God. I'm a simple wife and a mother who refused to let pain define me, who fought to arise after being knocked down, and as you read these pages, I want to encourage you that it is possible for you too.

In February 2024, I had the privilege of visiting Israel, where I stood at the very site of the pool of Bethesda—the site we read about in the gospel of John where Jesus healed the lame man. It was truly one of the most beautiful things I've ever seen, to be able to witness the place I had read about so many times in Scripture. Deep down in the earth, excavation had uncovered the very stone steps where Jesus once stood.

I imagined the crowd of people and pictured Jesus walking in and instantly changing the pain of someone who had been hurting for thirty-eight years. Together, in this book, we will turn to the Scriptures, to the stories of men and women God called to seasons of wilderness and suffering, and we'll see how He always had a plan of redemption for it all. The lame man at Bethesda had been waiting for almost four decades, lying by the pool in desperation, hoping for healing. And Jesus asked the man a simple question: "Do you want to be healed?" (John 5:6). Some translations say, "Do you want to be made well?"

That question isn't just for him—it's for me and for you. When we find ourselves on the bathroom floor, crushed by grief and feeling distant from God, this is the question we all must face: Do we truly want to be healed? Are we ready to surrender our pain; to expose our wounded, sinful hearts; and to trust Him—even when it's excruciating and nothing makes sense—so that Christ can begin His transforming work within us?

This book is my invitation to you. An invitation to arise, to pick up your mat, and to walk. Better yet, to *run*—to run the race set before you with endurance and hope, keeping your eyes on the Treasure. To find healing not from the world but from the Savior who meets you in your suffering. It hasn't been easy for me, and I'm certain it won't be easy for you, either, but nothing worth having ever is, and what can seem impossible for us is made possible through Jesus and His Word. There is a God who created you, who sees you, who gave His life for you, who is not surprised by your trials, and who is ready to meet you exactly where you are, to take your pain and, as you walk with Him, transform it into something beautiful for His glory.

So, friend, I ask you today: Do you want to be healed? Do you want to be made well?

Take my hand. Let's do this.

AFTER

One

THE BATHROOM

He drew me up from the pit of destruction, out of
the miry bog, and set my feet upon a rock, making
my steps secure.

Psalm 40:2

I sifted through clots of deep-red blood, searching for anything that would resemble the baby I was miscarrying. For hours I had lain sweating on the towel-covered cement floor of our bug-infested barn in the August heat of Texas. We had been living in an RV while our home was being built, and we had no plumbing in the fifth wheel, so my only place to go was the one barn bathroom we all shared.

The only position I could get comfortable in was on my hands and knees, curled in a ball. The pain was more intense than anything I'd ever felt, and I transitioned from crying to praying to—oddly—sleeping in between muscle contractions. Every two minutes, I would be in intense pain, then minor relief when I would fall asleep for a few moments. Occasionally my kids, London and Lincoln, would knock on the door.

"Mommy, are you okay? What's going on? What's taking so long in there?"

"I'm fine, baby. I'm just not feeling well," I would say through winced ache. I could tell when the next clot would be coming, so I would get up and move to the toilet. I caught the blood in my hands and searched for my baby. I knew, if anything, he would be so small I might miss him, but something about just letting him fall into the toilet to be flushed down the septic system made my heart sick. I thought, *Maybe if I see him, I can properly bury him.* I know that may sound strange and gross to so many, or maybe if you're a mother who has miscarried at home you've done the same thing I did.

I was nine weeks pregnant, and just four days before, at what was supposed to be my in vitro fertilization (IVF) graduation appointment, I was told crushing news about our little boy.

"Oh, Amber. I am so sorry. He no longer has a heartbeat."

My options given at the clinic were to go home and have the miscarriage naturally, to schedule and have a D&C (dilation and curettage), or to take medication to hurry the miscarriage along. I opted for the first. I knew just because the doctors said there was no heartbeat, God could still move. I left, hugging the nurses and holding back tears as I thanked them for everything they had done over the past year. With somber faces they offered their apologies. As I entered the elevator, I thought about how many times they have to give that heartbreaking news. I sat in the car in the parking garage and cried. I grabbed my phone to text my husband, Granger, who was about to leave for tour with his band.

"Have you left yet?"

"No, why?"

"I'm coming there."

I made the forty-minute drive from the Austin clinic to our family warehouse. *How could this be happening again?* I got out of the car and just shook my head. He knew and just hugged me. No tears from him. Just silence.

Our family had been through so much over the past few months. Just fourteen months before, we had buried our beautiful three-year-old redheaded baby boy, River, after he drowned in our backyard pool. We had been through two moves, a change of school for the kids, and COVID. Now we were losing another precious baby.

This time was different. I was hurt and grieving our little boy (we later named him Noah), but I was in a much different place mentally and spiritually. I had done the deep work of grief; I had fully surrendered my life to the Lord, and I trusted Him with this new heartbreak. After He had walked with me through all our suffering the past year and a half, I had full faith there was purpose in our pain, and I trusted that He would carry me through again.

On the morning the miscarriage naturally began, as I watched church online due to COVID, I felt the first cramps and knew it was time. I looked up and said, "Okay, Lord, I trust You." Then I got up, walked to the restroom, and prepared for what was coming. The miscarriage itself lasted about seven hours but didn't fully subside for three weeks. I never did see remnants of our baby, and I thank God for His grace in those moments.

If we live long enough in this fallen world, we will all face trials, pain, and suffering. No one is immune. It's not a matter of *if* but a matter of *when*. How do we begin to make sense of the awful things that happen? If God is good and loving, why do these things occur? How do we make the choice to keep going when all we want to do is throw in the towel?

How do we begin to find joy again when our hearts are shattered? I can't pretend to know your pain; each person's heartache and suffering are their own, and I can imagine you may have endured harder seasons than I have. But I can share my journey with you and tell you how God transformed my life by bringing me through something that almost killed us and using it to make us come alive in Him. He showed me that there is purpose in the hard things we must endure; that grief and joy can coexist; and that not only can you experience peace that surpasses understanding, even in your darkest moments, but you can live a more beautiful life than you ever thought possible by surrendering and trusting Him with it all.

I am not here to minimize your trials or tie a pretty bow around your suffering. I know this world is utterly tragic. This life can be so hard and so painful. And at times you will wrestle with not having answers for every question. But I am here to share with you what I have—what the gracious Lord has given me and offers to you: hope and joy and peace amid the heartache. You can be held together even when everything is falling apart.

You can be held together even when everything is falling apart.

I pray that, by the end of this book, you can see how good and gracious our Father is. I hope you can see that you are never alone, and I pray you will feel the joy I feel today that flows from the inside out. No matter how many tears you cry at night, joy can still come in the morning.

BEFORE

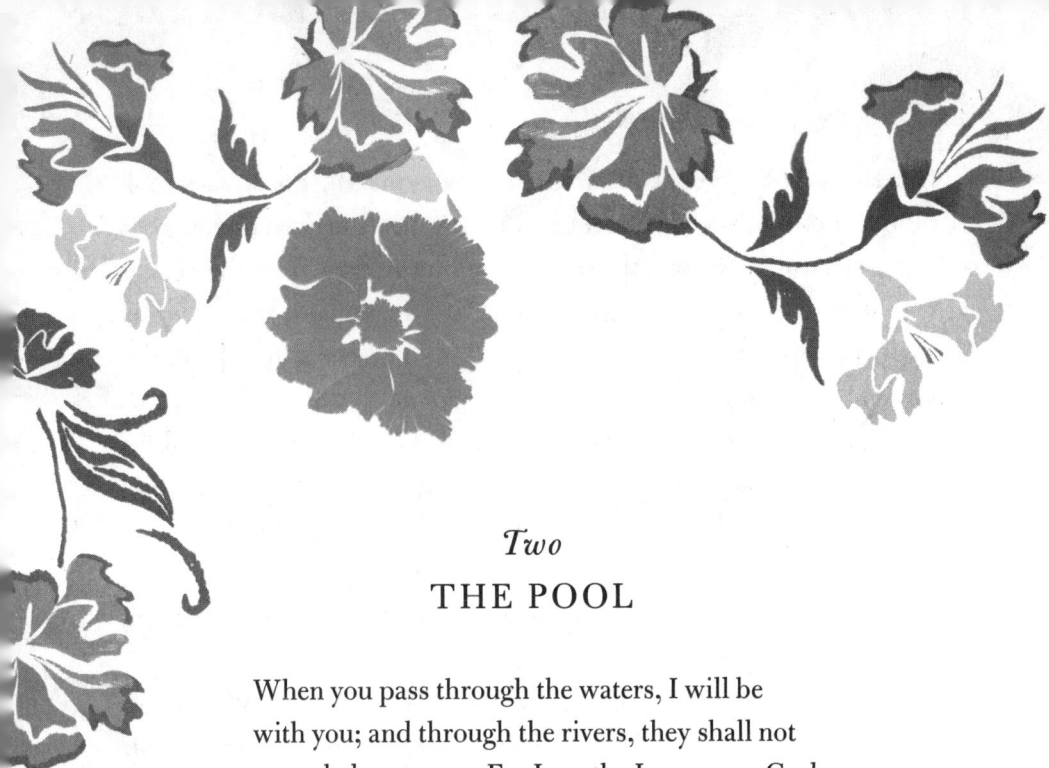

Two

THE POOL

When you pass through the waters, I will be
with you; and through the rivers, they shall not
overwhelm you. . . . For I am the Lord your God,
the Holy One of Israel, your Savior.

Isaiah 43:2–3

I had just gotten out of the shower and was sitting on the bed in our back bedroom when I heard muffled screaming coming from the other side of the house. All I could make out were the words *River* and *pool*. It took a moment for my mind to register what I'd just heard. Only about ten minutes earlier, my three children, London, Lincoln, and River, had gone outside with my husband, Granger. Dinner was finished and the kids were eager to play before bedtime.

Granger was leaving early in the morning for the CMT (Country Music Television) Music Awards, so they were spending some extra time together before he left. My daughter, London, wanted to show her daddy a new gymnastics routine she was making up, so they took off outside. Linc raced after them and little River begged to go too. It was a beautiful summer day in June, and it was normal for the kids to want to go out and play after dinner. Riv wiggled and kicked in his high chair in anticipation of following his siblings outside. I had the thought as I unbuckled him from his high chair, *Just put him to bed.* He was already in his new blue-and-white dino pj's he'd received for his third birthday just weeks before. But I allowed him to run outside and get any last wiggles out before bedtime. It had been a long day, I had been frustrated earlier with the kids fighting with one another, and, honestly, I welcomed the short break so I could take a quick shower.

After cleaning up the kitchen swiftly, I peeked outside. We had left the French doors open to let the warm breeze in as the kids played. The boys were annoying London, and when I glanced outside, Granger asked, "Can you please take the boys in?" My answer would haunt me for months. "I just need a quick break," I said.

Why did I take that break? Why didn't I just take them inside? Why didn't I just put River to bed? Why didn't I listen to that instinct? Instead, I headed back to take my shower. In motherhood, showers become speedy affairs. Usually, within a few seconds of going to the restroom or hopping in the shower, there are little fingers sliding under the door or sounds of knocking and loud cries of "Mama!" I've always felt I had to do everything rapidly and get back to my duties as a mom, so I always rushed through things I was doing for myself. So much so that when my mother-in-love would come help with the kids after I gave birth, she would say "It doesn't have to be quick" anytime I would ask, "Is it okay if I take a quick shower?"

My shower that night probably took six minutes at most, and as I sat on the bed after, those muffled words pierced through the opened doors, down the hall, to my room. I sprinted toward the commotion, panic and disbelief swirling in my mind. *Surely, I'm not hearing what*

I think I am. River *and* pool? *How? We have an iron gate. Everyone is outside. He must still be in the water. How did he get in the gate? This must have just happened. My poor baby must still be in the water waiting for someone to get him. I'm coming, River!*

I ran down the hall, and as I reached the patio, I screamed, "Where's Daddy?!" but as those words left my mouth, I saw him. Inside the locked pool gate was Granger, soaked and frantically trying to perform CPR on our lifeless son. My sweet redheaded boy whom I'd seen just moments ago, laughing and so excited to go outside, was now motionless on the concrete. I flung the gate open, and my first look was down at Riv. *No.* My heart shattered at the sight of his swollen, purple face. He was soaked, arms dangling, and his beautiful big brown eyes were bloodshot and wide open, rolling around as Granger held him. My eyes met Granger's for the first time. I've never seen such terror and helplessness in anyone's eyes before.

"Call 911! Go get your phone!" I immediately turned and darted back across the yard inside. *Phone, phone. Where the heck was my phone?* London ran back in with me and helped me in my frantic haze. Why when I needed it most could I not find it?! I found Granger's phone and quickly dialed 911 as I raced out through the patio doors back to the pool. What I said was a blur, something along the lines of "My son fell in the pool, he's isn't breathing, please help us!" The 911 operator calmly asked, "Do you know CPR?"

Granger, desperate and feeling defeated, confessed through exasperated breath, "No, I don't know what I'm doing." I remember yelling, "I do!" and I took over as the operator walked me through breaths and compressions.

I now know I didn't know what I was doing at all. All I knew was from the class I had taken in high school over twenty years ago. But when it's your own child, all calmness and recollection of technique go out the window. In my panic, I was breathing way too hard, focusing on the breaths and not the compressions. Terrified, I blew so hard into his little mouth, watching his stomach rise with each blow. Every time we would blow and compress, gushes of water and food would expel violently out of his mouth. In our naivete we thought we were making progress.

Breathe, compress, breathe, compress. We took turns while on the line with 911. I was covered in chlorinated water and vomit. Covered in macaroni and hot dogs from his lunch and dinner that day. *How is there so much water coming out of him? This isn't happening.* Minutes stretched endlessly as we struggled to revive him. London and Linc ran up at this point. Linc, eyes full of confusion and fear, asked, "Mommy, did River really fall in the pool? Did he really, Mommy?" His sweet little five-year-old mind couldn't comprehend what he was seeing. London just stood there stunned with her hands over her mouth. "Why are his cheeks purple, Mommy?"

We yelled at them to go inside as we kept at it. "Come on, baby. Please breathe, River. Please, God. Please wake up, baby." Still on the ground by the pool, I was scared to press too hard because his little head was on the cement. I didn't want to hurt him. But it didn't matter at this point. I knew when I had looked into River's eyes at that first glance that I had stared death in the face. The sound of pressing on his tiny body still haunts me. It was like the sound a boot full of water makes when you walk. *Swoosh, swoosh,* like a sponge. *Jesus.*

Minutes went by as we frantically tried to get our baby breathing. Lincoln came back down with a photo of River and said somberly, "At least I have a memory of him, Mommy." The innocence of a child. Granger and I locked eyes again. "Go inside, buddy!" He and London ran back in, and a few minutes later we finally heard sirens in the distance. *Thank God.* Little London, only seven, bravely ran out front to guide the parade of vehicles through our gate back to our pool.

The next moments were a blur. The EMTs rushed in and went to work on Riv. I saw my neighbor Roy run over and through our front door, his eyes wide. He heard the sirens and came running to our house. My sweet neighbor always checked on us. He knew Granger traveled a lot and he was always a phone call or text away when our water pipe burst or one of our crazy dogs escaped. Through heavy breaths I said, "River fell in the pool. He isn't breathing."

Police officers took us to the patio, sat us in chairs, and began their onslaught of routine questions. We just sat there wide-eyed, soaking wet, and in shock, staring into the distance. I don't even remember what they asked, but I do remember one officer looking me up and down, assessing me in my pink silk floral bathrobe and wet hair. Granger was in wet blue jeans and a T-shirt. There was a look of suspicion and almost disgust on one of their faces. We were now suspected criminals with a dead child, and I hadn't even had time to process what on earth was happening.

The EMTs said they had a pulse. *Oh, praise God*, we thought. As they told us they were taking him to the hospital, Granger yelled, "Well, let's go!" I rushed in to put on some dry clothes. Granger jumped in the car in the same wet clothes he was wearing and just slipped on his boots with no socks, which later caused huge blisters on his feet. I ran upstairs and told the kids to quickly get dressed.

"Come on, grab your shoes! We have to hurry!"

"What? Why? Where are we going?"

"Come on, hurry guys, they are taking River to the hospital. We have to go!"

I raced downstairs and threw on a green sweatshirt with holes in it and some pink cutoff shorts. I don't remember what shoes I grabbed, but as I turned the corner, I caught a glimpse of myself in the mirror. Red face, no makeup, wet hair that smelled of vomit, and a look of emptiness in my eyes. I thought, *Why are you looking at yourself in the mirror?! There is no time for that!* I raced outside and we jumped in the car. In my shock I didn't try to get into the ambulance. I don't know why. The officers stayed back at the house. Our quiet country home was now a crime scene. As we left, the officers asked if there were any weapons inside. We said yes, told them where, and followed the ambulance out. River couldn't be medevaced that day. The helicopter they normally use was grounded due to a storm coming, so it wasn't available. Of course it wasn't.

On our drive, our friend Price, a local fireman, called. He had been at another station when someone came in talking about a call and said, "That call is from your boy's house."

"Who?" he asked.

"Granger's."

As I picked up the phone, he calmly but with urgency and compassion in his voice told me they were diverting River to another hospital. Price later told me he was so scared to make that call. So worried about what we were going through on the other end of it. He said his heart was beating out of his chest. But in a moment of panic and horror, it was comforting to hear the calm voice of someone we knew. Word began to get out. Because Granger was a touring musician, he was well-known in the area, and he always had good relationships with law enforcement and first responders who looked out for our family. We drove 90 to nothing, all of us asking each other questions at the same time.

"When was the last time you saw him?"

"How did he get in the gate?"

"Did anyone see anything?"

"How long was he in the water?"

"How long was the gymnastics routine?"

"Mommy, is he going to be okay? Is River going to die?"

Granger said, "Bubby is going to be very sick, but they got his heartbeat back. He is going to be okay, guys. Let's pray."

Up to this point the sky had been beautiful and blue, sun shining, when suddenly a storm came out of nowhere. As we drove, the skies turned dark gray and the clouds opened and began to pour. Huge, heavy drops of rain pounded the windshield, making it hard to see as we darted around traffic on the highway.

Rain had always had a special meaning in our family. It had rained the day I met Granger, the day we got engaged, our wedding day, and each of the days the kids were born. Now it was raining the day our three-year-old son drowned. We could barely see through the windshield as we sped in and out of lanes with our flashers on.

We made it to the first hospital, beating the ambulance. They brought us into a small waiting area and began asking us questions. Something inside my body flipped on itself and I was in intense pain. It felt like an organ, like my stomach or intestines had cramped and were turning upside down. I bent over in agony for a few minutes and breathed through the ache. It subsided after a bit, and they allowed us into the ER where they were working on Riv.

He was naked, the room was bright white and warm, and there were probably five to ten people racing around, calling out medical codes and numbers as they worked. I heard one doctor say, "He's fighting." To me, that meant that our sweet Riv was fighting to breathe, that maybe he was coming back. Maybe he really was going to be okay. Granger and I stood in the corner of the room helpless. I silently cried into his shoulder, my back to the rest of the room. Partly because I couldn't bear to watch what was happening to my precious baby, partly due to the shame I was already feeling that we had let this happen.

It was determined that River needed specialized care and had to be transferred to Dell Children's Medical Center in Austin, Texas. Once again, we raced through the storm to meet the ambulance at the new hospital where we would spend the next three agonizing days.

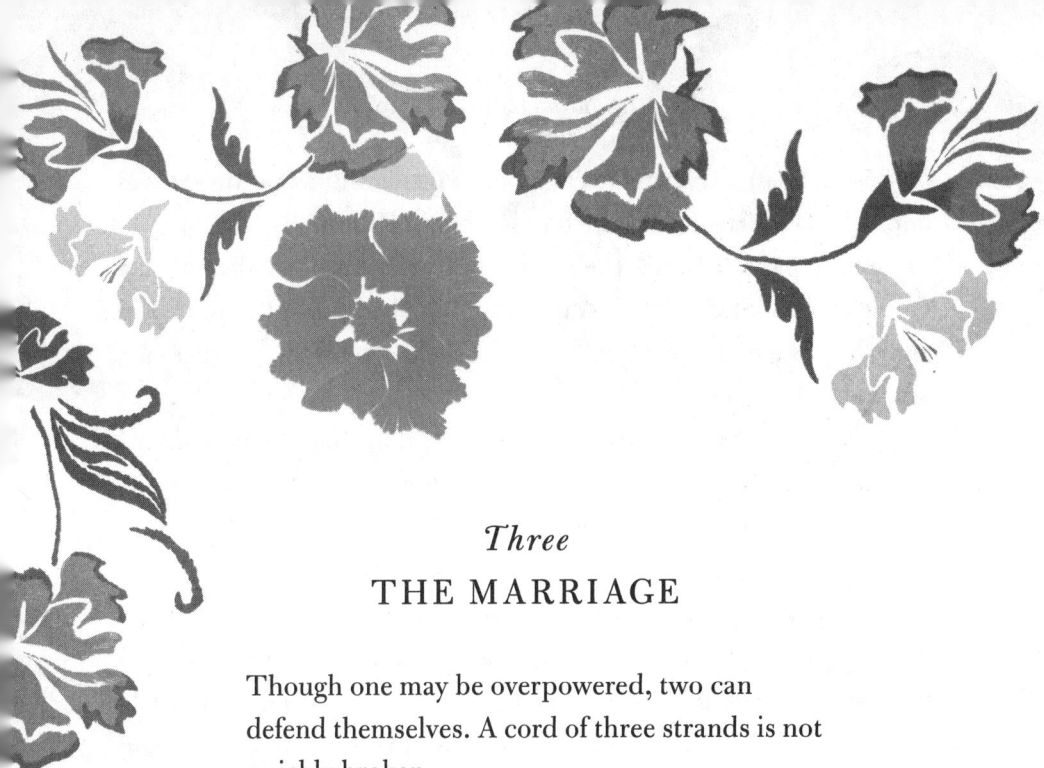

Three

THE MARRIAGE

Though one may be overpowered, two can
defend themselves. A cord of three strands is not
quickly broken.

Ecclesiastes 4:12 NIV

Granger and I met in the winter of 2009. He was a singer-songwriter
living in College Station, Texas, and I was a part-time actor working
in commercials, music videos, and low-budget movies living in my
hometown of Fort Worth. Our first connection came via Facebook,
when Granger messaged me one evening about an audition for a new
music video. They had just completed a round of auditions and made
the selection for his love interest. But when he got home, he didn't
feel right about that choice. As he was online that evening, my picture
popped up on the "people you may know" tab, and he later told me he
thought, *That's the girl.* We chatted a few times through Messenger,
and I decided, Why not? It could be another fun thing to add to

my résumé. After a few conversations and the initial audition, I was booked for his first music video to be shot in Killeen, Texas.

Accompanied by my best friend, Christine, for safety, I met Granger at the Starbucks in Waco. Thinking back now, I would never allow my daughter to go meet strangers she'd met on the internet for a video shoot, but I digress.

It was a drizzly day, and as I shook the rain from the hood of my gray zip sweatshirt while entering the coffee shop, our eyes met for the first time. He was wearing blue jeans, a T-shirt, and a ball cap, and as he stood up to greet me, his smile captivated me. I felt something I wasn't expecting. *Whoa, that was weird*, I thought. After saying hello to his brother Tyler, my friend and I ordered our coffee and went into the restroom, gossiping about the brothers. Granger had long, curly brown hair that flipped out under his ball cap and kind, deep brown eyes—eyes that smiled while resting, the same eyes as our sweet little Riv would have one day. And I knew I was in trouble.

The day was filled with scenes set up of a couple in love, making chocolate chip cookies, dancing to country songs on the patio, a glass of red wine and a bubble bath, kissing under the sheets, and even sharing our first fight—one that was staged and is still one of the only true-blue, all-out fights we've ever had. I know that may seem hard to believe, but he and I just don't fight. I've really been so grateful for our patience and kindness with each other over the past fifteen years. I knew when I left that evening that I had to see him again. My friend tried to talk me down from the immense high that I was on. "You were acting. You don't really have feelings for him. Anyone who acted like that all day would think they liked that person."

"No, it's different," I said. "Something is different." I had just started dating someone a couple of months before, someone I did really like, so the feelings I felt that day for Granger really caught me off guard, and this encounter ended up changing the trajectory of my life. I waited a few days to see if what I felt was real, but I couldn't shake the need to see him again. So, I texted him one day and asked if he by chance felt anything that I felt that day.

"Hey, I wanted to ask you something. Were we just acting, or did you feel something that day too?" I texted.

Being the gentleman that he is, he texted back, "Well, regardless of how you feel about me, it's probably more of an indication that you need to break up with that guy."

Oof. He was right.

After some hard conversations, I did. A few weeks went by, and Granger texted me again and said, "Hey, I'm playing a show in Waxahachie. Would you be interested in meeting for a cup of coffee after I finish?"

"Hey you! Sure, what time?"

We met late that evening, sipped coffee, and spent hours just talking and laughing together. We closed down Starbucks, and the rest is history. He later told me that during the video shoot he could tell I was acting on the first two takes of our kiss. "But the second two," he said, "those were real."

We got engaged six months later in the rain in York, England, in front of the beautiful York Minster Cathedral, and were married six months after that in a cold, rainy February ceremony with fifty of our closest friends and family by our side in Horseshoe Bay, Texas.

I didn't know much about life and career goals back then other than knowing I wanted to be a mother. During our engagement we always said we wanted "three plus one" anytime we talked about having children. The "plus one" was leaving the door open to adoption or fostering someday. Or so we thought. Our first year of marriage was blissful. It was almost as if we were living out that music video in real time. I realize the first year for some isn't always easy. There are lots of changes happening. You are learning to share space with each other, making financial decisions together, navigating expectations and conflict; but unbeknownst to us, our trials would come later.

Early on, we enjoyed lazy mornings and late nights, and sipped vanilla whiskey and Coke while wrapped in each other's arms watching silly shows on TV. On the weekends, I would travel with Granger and the guys across Texas and Oklahoma as he played shows to empty bars and smoke-filled clubs. I sold his merch some nights with my brother-in-law Tyler, and we would often compete for who could make the most money on a given night.

Those are nights I'll always remember. I loved my time with the band in those van and trailer days. Lots of miles, long shows, gas station stops, hilarious jokes—and falling deeper in love with him with every highway mile. I always told people it would have been difficult if I didn't like his music, but thankfully, I loved it. I loved watching him perform onstage. I loved seeing him in his element. He had such talent and stage presence. I was like a giddy schoolgirl every time he performed. My mom used to say some of the best parts of the shows were watching me watch him on that stage.

We started our family a year into our marriage. We had our plan. We'd try for our first child and then aim to space them out every two years after that. By God's grace, we were blessed with our beautiful daughter, London, in 2011. She was named after my European ancestry. My grandmother, whom I called Nanny, grew up in London and later moved to the States after she met my granddad while he was serving in the US Air Force in the 1950s.

Sweet little Lincoln came in 2014, named after Lincolnshire (staying with the British theme), and our redheaded River showed up in all his chunky glory weighing in at 9 pounds, 10 ounces, in May of 2016. We actually just simply loved the name River; in fact, if London had been a boy, we would have chosen that name, but there is the River Thames in London, so we were still in the British motif.

He was the only baby I ever felt contractions with. The morning of my scheduled cesarean I woke in the middle of the night to painful contractions two minutes apart. He was right on time and moving fast, something that followed him all the days of his short life. I opted to have my fallopian tubes tied after Riv was born. After three cesareans due to carrying my babies breech in the womb, we thought it would be better, per the doctor's advice, for me to have the tubal ligation during the delivery procedure.

Everything in our plan was going accordingly. Life was good. Hard—in the ordinary ways of caring for three tiny humans with a husband on the road a lot—but good.

Granger's touring picked up around this time, and he was gone as many as 250 days some years. Having three kids under five with a traveling husband wasn't always the easiest. Someone always needed me. One baby might be crying or hungry or hurt, or on occasion, they all were; or one was sick and I was scrambling to quarantine and keep the others from getting sick; or we were all sick and I was running back and forth to each of their rooms cleaning throw-up and changing diapers and sheets in the middle of the night, while simultaneously running to the restroom to be sick myself.

I always felt like I needed four extra arms and much more time in the day. There was never enough of me to go around. I would often say, "One mommy, three babies—you gotta have some patience with me," when they were pulling at me for different things. I felt mom guilt that I wasn't giving each of them the love and attention they all needed, but I was darn sure doing my best. All of this definitely gave way to some tears and exhaustion at times. There was very little sleep during those early years. I would hide in my bathroom or closet some days and cry from being overwhelmed with the daily duties of motherhood and feeling like I was failing. I realize some of you women do this with seven children or more. You are superheroes in my book!

Even with all the sickness, tears, feeling overwhelmed, and lack of sleep, I wouldn't trade those days for anything. We played, we made messes, we explored, we ate tons of ice cream, we said "I love you" and gave each other kisses multiple times a day, we created, we danced on the kitchen table. We really did enjoy every minute of our sweet little life. Our marriage was great, our babies were healthy, Granger's career was booming, and we had the little farmhouse on a piece of land at the end of a gravel drive. We even had the white picket fence. Life by most people's standards was ideal. And then it wasn't.

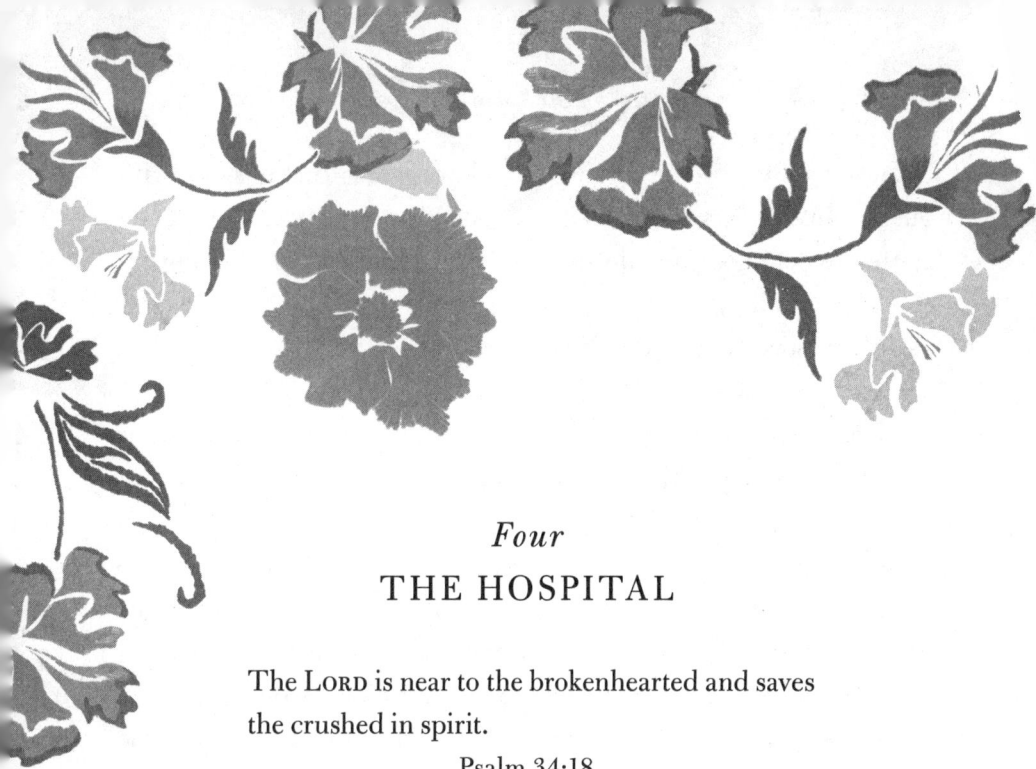

Four

THE HOSPITAL

The LORD is near to the brokenhearted and saves
the crushed in spirit.

Psalm 34:18

As we got settled into the room at Dell Children's, our "bigs" as we call them, London and Lincoln, went home with our friends Heidi and Caleb for the evening. We hadn't notified anyone yet, but Caleb was friends with a local officer who had called him to see if we were okay after the officer had heard about the incident. So our friends immediately reached out and came to help. The hospital was so kind and caring, giving the kids popsicles and teddy bears to calm their nerves, but I later learned that London was pretty worked up and got sick on the side of the road on the way home. She still won't touch blue Powerade to this day because it's what she was drinking the night River drowned.

We sent the kids home and still hadn't called our family yet because we thought for sure we would be leaving that hospital with our son in tow in a matter of hours. At this point River's tiny body started twitching off and on, and we asked the nurses in eager hope if this was a good sign.

"Any movement is good," we were told.

We kept praying.

I feel the need to stop here and tell you I was not a Christ follower at this point in my life. I had grown up going to an Episcopal church some Sundays in my adolescence, but I had never had a relationship with Jesus. After my parents divorced when I was four, my mom tried to keep the foundation of church going, but it later fizzled in the wake of my brother's youth soccer and strange men at church overstepping boundaries with Mom, making her uncomfortable during service.

I was a very lost teenager and young adult. I think I rebelled due to the divorce and some things that happened to me when I was little. On more than one occasion, I had been sexually molested by people I knew. I never shared that information with my parents or anyone else. I don't think I processed it fully until I was in my thirties. My rebellion wasn't your typical loud, in-your-face variety, though; it was more done in secret.

On the surface, I was a good student, made good grades, was a cheerleader and tennis player, and had lots of friends, but behind the scenes I began seeking acceptance and love in all the wrong places. I was never taught my worth or value as a young girl, and the pain of divorce and loss of innocence carved a path that led to promiscuity and abusive relationships, both verbally and physically. I longed to feel loved, especially from boys. I got secret tattoos, partied with friends, and made some really terrible, sinful choices that left lasting scars on my heart, making me believe I could never be accepted, loved, or forgiven by God.

Granger was raised in a home rooted in faith, with parents who admit they weren't perfect and that any good they did was from the

24

Lord, but they were dedicated to instilling Christian values. His mother showed her devotion early on by reading the entire New Testament to him as she nursed him. Granger and his brothers were involved in church and Christian Young Life groups, but he, too, will tell you he wasn't walking fully with Jesus.

When Granger and I met, I remember feeling so intimidated by his mom, Debbee. Not in the physical sense or in any way she treated me. She's small and adorably sweet, measuring in at five foot two. But she had such strong faith. It was something I didn't quite understand, and it made me feel insecure in a way, like maybe I could never measure up. She spoke of Jesus and the Bible in ways I had never heard before. She just truly loved the Lord, and it showed. Granger and I spoke about church on occasion and about wanting to give our children a foundation of faith, but it would be years before we took the steps to make that happen.

Around the same time a sweet friend from a mom's club kept inviting me to her church, but I would make excuses as to why I couldn't go.

"I don't want to go without Granger, and he's always gone on tour Sundays."

"It will be too hard with three little kids."

"The church is just too large for us."

I wonder if you've done the same thing. How long has God been putting people in your life, planting seeds, pursuing, knocking, inviting you to draw near to Him, and you've responded with reasons to keep Him at arm's length?

Maybe you've thought, *I'll start going to church once my schedule clears up.* Or *I just don't have the energy right now.* Or *I can't go to church, I've sinned too much for God to ever accept me.* Or even *I don't need to go to church to have a relationship with Jesus.*

Why do we do this? Why do we hesitate to open the door when God, in His tender mercy, is offering us something far better than the perceived comfort of staying where we are?

The truth is, we don't have to clean ourselves up before coming to Him. If we keep waiting, there will always be another excuse, and as I've learned, tomorrow isn't guaranteed. God invites us to come. That's the call. Come and see. Don't let fear or pride or comfort or shame keep hardening your heart and locking the door that the Lord is beckoning you to enter.

In the summer of 2017, we experienced a terrifying scare with River. Blood work had come back with results suggesting a rare form of blood cancer, and the first moment I can remember truly crying out to God came after I hung up from that phone call. I remember it like it was yesterday. It was a Wednesday morning in July, around ten o'clock. I hit my knees on the cold beige tiles of my bathroom floor, gripping the edge of the sink as I fell. Through tears, I cried out, "Please, God. Oh, God, please don't let this be true. I will do anything. I will give you my life. Please, Jesus, help my baby." I pleaded over and over.

That desperate prayer on my knees was the beginning of something new in me—a heart that, for the first time, was humbled knowing this was completely out of my hands. I needed God. I had no control over this. And I begged that He would hear my cries. I called Granger after my prayer, and we called family and friends to pray for little Riv. The next morning, still worried, we returned to the doctor for more blood work. To my overwhelming relief, the tests showed no sign of cancer. *Wow.*

There is a story in Scripture about King Hezekiah. He was faced with a terminal illness and told by the prophet Isaiah to set his house in order, for he was going to die. Heartbroken, like me, Hezekiah turned to the Lord, praying with all his heart. God heard his desperate cry and, in His mercy, granted Hezekiah fifteen more years of life (Isaiah 38).

I like to believe that God, just as He did with Hezekiah, heard my plea on that bathroom floor and, for reasons I may never fully understand, gave us three more precious years with River. That gift became the beginning of my journey toward Him, a path that would slowly draw me closer. From that day forward, I stopped with the excuses. I sought the God I had cried out to. I accepted my friend's invitation to attend her church one Sunday—the kids loved it, and so did I. I began attending Christian women's conferences, joined local Bible studies, read devotionals, and listened to worship music on repeat.

True faith involves repenting of sin, trusting in Jesus, and dying to yourself daily.

It felt good, like I was finally starting to do the things I needed to do to build this foundation we were seeking. But in reality, I still wasn't living a life fully surrendered to Jesus.

True faith involves repenting of sin, trusting in Jesus, and dying to yourself daily, but back then, I was still living for me, for my comfort, for my pleasure. I wasn't reading my Bible. I continued to look to the world for fulfillment, joy, and peace. Real surrender—the true death to self—would come only through the deepest pain I could imagine, a pain I hope never to experience again.

A Dire Turn

At 9 p.m. two years later we knew River was facing a much more serious situation than we could have imagined. The little movements and twitches he was experiencing were the start of seizures throughout his tiny body. He began to seize so hard they had to put a little rubber piece in his mouth so he wouldn't bite his tongue. EEG monitors were placed all throughout his beautiful red hair with glue to monitor brain activity. I can still smell that glue today.

Granger and I walked outside of the big sliding hospital doors, past the officer who was still there to ask us questions, and we each called our parents to break the news. We assured them that River would be okay, but we wanted to let them know what was going on. Sensing our fear and urgency, our parents all came as quickly as they could to be with us. My heart broke more with every second. I retreated often to the bathroom down the long hall past the other rooms on the second floor over the next twelve hours, sometimes feeling like I would be sick, other times just to silently cry.

I chose the bathroom farthest away from everyone else but still on the same floor of the PICU closest to River so I could be completely alone. I entered the single bathroom and locked the door behind me. *God, why is this happening?* Looking up, with closed eyes and winced face as I began to cry, I slid my back down the white wall until I settled onto the sterile purple tile floor next to the toilet. The air smelled of alcohol and air freshener. I wrapped my arms around my knees and buried my head in between.

"Oh, River, I am so sorry." Tears streamed down my face. "God, please heal my baby. Please. Please bring him back to us." I begged God for miracles in that tiny room. I hid from everyone else and from the heartbreaking reality down the long hall. I didn't see it then, but the bathroom was becoming my sanctuary of sorts. It would be the place God met me each and every time. It would be where I surrendered it all to Him and where He called me to arise.

Granger and I didn't sleep at all over those next few days. The staff kept encouraging us to drink a little water or at least eat a cracker to maintain our own sanity and not succumb to exhaustion and pass out through this harrowing ordeal, but even sipping water was difficult. I couldn't think about eating or drinking while my baby was lifeless, hooked up to machines with monitors and wires and IVs all over his little body. Not to mention we were constantly being pulled away from him by police officers and child protective services at all hours of that first long, dark night, being questioned about the most horrific event of our lives. It was all too much to handle. I just wanted to lie down with River. I wanted our sweet, wild boy to wake up, and I wanted life to go back to normal. At one point a chaplain arrived to talk with us. I remember thinking, *Why on earth is a chaplain here? Don't they come when people die?* River wasn't going to die. Was he?

Our family and friends had arrived late in the evening, and we all prayed and cried together. We would take turns whispering to River and kissing his precious ivory face, rosy cheeks, and chubby fingers. He looked perfect. As if he were only comfortably sleeping. He was tucked under his monogrammed blue blanket, his favorite red Lightning McQueen car placed gently in his hand. River loved that blanket, and it was always to be placed just right with the monogram at the bottom or he would make you fix it or get frustrated and fix it himself.

"No, this way, Mama!" he would squeal.

In the morning as I was coming back from a cry session in the bathroom, I caught a glimpse of the doctor down the hall. He was laughing and smiling with another nurse. It infuriated me. How could he be so callous? Didn't he know how much pain we were in? Didn't he know our son was dying in the room across from him? Grief will do that to you. It wasn't his fault my son was lifeless. It wasn't his trauma. He was just at work, doing his job, trying to help everyone on that floor. I couldn't expect him to feel what we were feeling—he saw this kind of thing every day—but it still stung. I walked past him into the family waiting room they had for us, and he entered behind me to give us some news about River's EEG and brain activity.

"I've read a lot of literature and I've seen a lot of patients—I'm so sorry," he said with glassy eyes as he sat down.

I secretly wondered how he went from smiling to glassy eyes so quickly.

"There is zero chance your son will recover. He is the closest to brain-dead that he can be, and he's heading in that direction."

"Wait, what?! *Zero* chance?!" I put my head back between my knees. "What do you mean zero chance?" I questioned as I looked up.

the girl *on the* bathroom floor

This made no sense. How was there no chance? Not 1 percent, not half a percent? Give me something! I wanted to scream. I knew River was sick, and we had been told that if he woke up he may have some brain injuries or learning disabilities we would have to work through, but I never thought there would be zero chance of recovery. How could this prognosis have already been made? We had been here less than twelve hours. It all seemed so quick for them to have come to that conclusion already.

"River will not recover from this. I am so sorry."

The room was still. All our family sat trying to process the news. After a few silent moments, Granger looked the doctor in the eyes and asked, "If this was your son, what would you do?"

"I would stop," he said as a tear rolled down his cheek. Up to this point Riv had PICC lines placed and was being pumped full of medicine to keep his little body stable and his heart pumping.

We were now faced with the decision of when to unplug the machines that were keeping him alive. How did my sweet, smiling son go from laughing and playing just twelve hours before to zero chance of him ever opening his eyes again? Granger's brother Tyler chimed in from the corner of the room, "Wait, this is Riv we're talking about here!" River was always a fighter. He held his own with his brother and sister in any sort of battle or wrestling match. He always went hard and fast. He wasn't scared of anything, and he kept me on my toes as I would find him climbing on the outside of stair banisters all the way to the top or darting in and around trees in his favorite green-and-yellow John Deere tractor. Anytime he did something dangerous, and I would scold him and tell him to stop or get down or be careful, he would always smile at me with a mischievous look, push his pointer finger hard into the tip of his nose, and say, "Shhh, it's okay, Mama." He was full of fire and life and joy. He was our little fighter. Surely, he would recover. Surely, they were wrong. We just needed a second opinion.

"Of course, we will bring in another team and have them assess," the doctor said as he left the room.

I cried as I walked back to the room and slowly climbed into the bed with River, whispering words of encouragement in his ear that I secretly somehow knew were words of farewell. "Baby, if you can fight, fight and come back to us, but if you can't, I can give you back. I don't want to, but I can. I'm so thankful you were mine. I'm so, so sorry, Riv. I love you so much."

Those words just rolled out of my mouth without a thought. What kind of mother was I? I could *give you back*? Give you back where? It was the beginning of the realization that all of this was bigger than what was happening in this room. There was a strange peace when there should have been none. Granger would later tell me he felt that same peace. The doctors and nurses said they had never seen a family with such peace and so unified, trusting, and calm in the face of unthinkable pain. It absolutely wasn't our own strength. We were not alone in that room, and there was something much bigger directing our steps and holding our shattered hearts as we made the decisions that were unthinkable.

Exhausted from crying and prayer, Granger and I lay together on the makeshift bed opposite River and drifted in and out of moments of sleep. Every few minutes the nurses would come in to administer medicine or take vitals, the constant beeps of the monitors never allowing for rest or reprieve from the nightmare. When the second evening came, the head of neurology met with us and confirmed our worst fears. River had no brain activity. Our baby boy would never recover.

Granger walked over to River after the news was given to us and slowly lifted River's eyelids. "Come here, babe. Come look. He's gone." I walked over and looked into River's eyes. Eyes that were once so full of life and mystery. People always said there was something different about his eyes. They were deep, dark chocolate brown, almost black. Eyes that would pierce through your soul when he looked at you. It was as if he knew something you didn't. He used to grab my face with his tiny hands, look deep into my eyes, and say, "I love you so much, Mama!" Words that went straight to my heart. And now those gorgeous deep brown eyes were empty and lifeless. My sweet boy. I didn't want to believe it, but it was something I somehow already knew. I knew River wasn't in that room with us. I knew he was gone. Seeing the emptiness in those eyes only helped to confirm what the doctors had told us and what we were already feeling.

Even though I knew in my heart that it was just the machines keeping River alive, I still wrestled and struggled with the thought, *What if the doctors are wrong? What if we let go too soon? What if he just needs more time?* With every little movement on the monitor I would question if it was River coming back or just another seizure. But in those moments of wrestling, like lightning, I was hit with the thought of organ donation. River's little body was perfect. Everything except his brain was operating as it should. If we had to say goodbye, how could we say goodbye and bury him if he could potentially help someone else?

I'd known I wanted to be an organ donor from my youth. *If I were to pass*, I always thought, *why would I go into the ground with perfectly good organs that could help bring life to another?* I just never envisioned having to make that decision for my child. This was all cruelly out of order. This was all so wrong. It wasn't something we had discussed, but to Granger's surprise, I brought up organ donation to the nurses in the room. This bought us a little more time with him as they called in the donor team and began compiling the paperwork and searching for recipients. If we couldn't receive our miracle of healing and bring River home, I wanted someone else to receive theirs and be able to bring their baby home. This was the beginning of seeing a glimmer of light and purpose in our darkest time. The beginning of feeling that this awful pain wasn't all for nothing.

So often in suffering we can ask the universal questions: Where are you, God? Why me? Why does a good God allow so much pain and heartache? These are all natural questions in our finite minds here on earth. We don't want pain. We try to avoid it at all costs. We want happy, healthy lives. We want comfort and pleasure, smooth sailing and joy. I don't know what trial you are facing right now, and I don't know what heartache you will endure in the future, but I do know that suffering is inevitable.

Just in the time I have written the manuscript for this book, in my friend circle alone, I have a girlfriend walking through divorce because her husband decided he wasn't happy anymore, so he had an affair and left her and their two little girls to pick up the pieces. Another dear friend had to watch both of her parents' bodies be ravaged by cancer. They died within months of each other, after they had already lost her sister to the same disease a few years before. This same friend just recently lost her grandmother as well, and she struggles with difficulties in her marriage. One friend is navigating healing from sexual trauma after being date-raped. My son's best friend, only ten years old, just had surgery to remove a rare tumor. I have friends battling suicide of loved ones, self-harm, adultery, chronic daily pain, addiction, caring for brain-injured children day in and day out, miscarriage and child loss, losing everything to a house fire. The list of sorrows is endless.

We live in a world marred by sin and sickness and death, and while I don't know the specific hurt you are experiencing, I do know the feeling of having your heart ripped out of your chest. I know the feeling of trying to bring your dead child back to life. I know the feeling of lying on the bathroom floor, feeling so alone, and crying so hard that no more tears will come out. I know the pain of having to pick out a tiny casket and burial clothes for your baby and telling his brother and sister that their best friend is never coming home.

I know this life can be devastating, but I also know that God is good. And this isn't just something that Christians say. This is something I have come to know is true by walking through my darkest time. This is something I now believe to my core. I want to show you how the most painful season of my life gave way to new life and new joy I never imagined, and how, if you find yourself on the bathroom floor, the same can be true for you.

It wasn't an easy road. It was messy and hard. It took a lot of work, a lot of tears, and a lot of surrender. But I stand here five years later a new woman. A woman completely broken and rebuilt. A woman refined by the sovereign hand and grace of our good God. A woman who has been given a new song of praise in her mouth. My prayer is for you to know this Jesus. The One who said, "In this world you will have trouble. But take heart! I have overcome the world" (John 16:33 NIV). The One who said, "Fear not, for I am with you" (Isaiah 41:10). The One who came to save and redeem. I want you to know the God of the Bible. I want you to live with assurance that He is for you, that you are not alone, and that your story isn't over. When everything seems to be falling apart, it may actually be falling right into place.

When everything seems to be falling apart, it may actually be falling right into place.

Five

THE UNTHINKABLE

The LORD gave, and the LORD has taken away;
blessed be the name of the LORD.

Job 1:21

*Late into the night of day two in the hospital we were told the trans-*plant team had found recipients for River's organs. Surgery would be in just a few hours, and we had to say our goodbyes. We wanted each family member to have private time with Riv up until it was time for his procedure. One by one, faced with the reality of the finality of what was imminent, the people who loved River the most were forced to do something no one wanted.

Each person had been grieving in their own way over the last thirty-six hours. My mom had been hysterically crying, devastated and so angry. She went into the chapel of the hospital and was wailing so loudly she knew everyone could hear her. She then had to break the news to my little brother, who was serving time in prison. Feeling stuck, helpless, and crying on the other end of the phone, he yelled, "I have to get out of here! I have to get out of here!" He was unable to be with us and instead grieved alone in his small and empty jail cell. My mother-in-love wept and fervently prayed to the Lord, trying to comfort her sons and everyone else in the room. Just five years earlier she had lost the love of her life, her husband of thirty-seven years (thirty-seven years, five months, and two days to be exact), to a sudden heart attack, and now she was losing her precious grandbaby.

The uncles, Parker and Tyler, seemed more internal and stoic, as men often do, and I never got to see their private grief or what it entailed. My best friend of over twenty years, Christine—the one who was with me when Granger and I met, the one who stood beside me on our wedding day and held each of our babies when they were born—had been on a trip with friends out of the country when she got the call. Without hesitation, she jumped on a flight in the middle of the night and flew back to Texas to be with us. She couldn't cry out of her shock and trying to be strong for me, but she curled up at the foot of River's hospital bed, with her hands gripping my legs as I slept with Riv.

My mom, who sat in the chair across from us, witnessed this beautiful display of friendship in heartbreak—something she would talk about for years. I remember my sweet bonus dad being so overcome with emotion after he said his goodbye that he forced his way out, flinging open the door to River's hospital room, sobbing down the hall. Dan loved us and had raised us as if we were his own. He adored his grandkids, and this was all too much. It broke me to see that this pain wasn't only affecting us. It was crushing the hearts of everyone who loved our son.

About 10:45 a.m. on June 6, it was time for the honor walk, where nurses and doctors and family and friends line the halls as a loved one is wheeled into surgery to give life to another. We somberly followed as they pushed Riv's bed down the hall. I had trouble looking anyone in the eye, but I did lock eyes with my mom as we walked by. I could feel the ache between us. Grief and shame can feel a lot alike, and I was feeling both in that moment. We asked the nurses for one more favor. The staff over those three days had been so kind and tender. They'd cried with us, spoken gently to River as if he were still there with us, when we knew only his earthly body was in the room. They would talk to him so sweetly and were so tender anytime they moved him or rolled him or gave him medicine or took vitals.

"Hey, buddy, I'm gonna roll you over real quick," they would whisper. Or "Hey, sweet boy, I'm just going to check this line right here and make sure it's still good."

They loved him and treated us as if we were the only ones there, though we know every room had a family hurting just as much as we were—evident by the guttural cries of other grief-stricken moms and dads we could hear through the walls during our stay.

"Everything River did in his life was fast. Could you push him fast one last time?" Granger said, with tears in his eyes.

The thought of them pushing him fast down that hall, giving him one last ride, still brings me to tears. We smiled for the first time in three days as those four wheels rolled past the line of nurses who had cared for him. Our family and friends looking on with the saddest faces but also looks of solidarity in their eyes. When we came to the end of the hall, we both kissed him one more time, they pushed his bed through the big double doors, and then . . . they closed. That was the last time I ever saw my son.

Granger and I stood there silent. I would ache for months when we got home because I didn't hold him one last time before he went in for surgery. I was too afraid to hurt him. He had so many wires and things attached to him that I was afraid I would mess something up. All I did was lie beside him, kissing his little cheeks and hands, toes and chest. How stupid of me to not hold my baby. One thing the Enemy will do in grief is make you question everything you did. You will replay all the what-ifs over and over. You will have regrets and thoughts that you should have prayed harder or waited longer or done more.

I would often see and read stories of other children drowning after River died, and I would find myself checking for updates at all times of the day and night, wondering if their child had made any progress, opened their eyes, or miraculously survived. I saw stories of other couples who seemed to pray harder or wait longer, and I would drive myself crazy as I second-guessed everything we did. Sidenote here—don't do that to yourself. Comparison will keep you stuck in a cycle of anger and bitterness.

Comparison will keep you stuck in a cycle of anger and bitterness.

There were some occasions where the child did miraculously survive with no apparent lasting injury. Those gutted me. I was so happy for them, and I honestly had prayed for their healing because I knew the pain they were walking through, but I couldn't understand why their child came back and River didn't. But then there were other families whose children did open their eyes again, and while they were able to take their babies home, the children now live with traumatic brain injuries and need round-the-clock care. I can't tell you why God allows what He does, but I can tell you that the Enemy is a liar and a deceiver, and his goal is to keep you in the bondage of shame, guilt, regret, and questioning God's goodness. That wasn't the last time the Enemy would attack us as we walked this painful road.

While River was in surgery, Granger and I stepped into the outdoor area named the "Healing Garden" by the hospital. A sweet, serene place with beautiful, lush trees and brightly colored flowers and ponds filled with fish. He and I hadn't really talked much our whole time in the hospital. We were just a comfort to each other in our shock and pain, often holding each other without words. But here, overlooking the koi pond, we looked into each other's eyes and vowed to not let this tear our family apart. Our son was dying, but our marriage would not. We would not become a statistic. We would fight for the good through this pain and search for purpose and meaning in it. When we said "I do," we meant it. For better or for worse. And this was the worst.

We walked back into the hospital room hand in hand. All our family was seated on the floor. The room was a mess with bags and gifts and blankets. I said through tears to our family, "Please don't be mad at us. I am so sorry." I was so sorry that we had allowed this to happen. That we had broken their hearts as well as our own. That we had failed to keep River safe. That we had to be the ones to make the decision to say goodbye. Of course, in their kindness, they assured us they weren't mad at us. That this was all a terrible tragedy.

Moments later the surgeon came into the room and confirmed River's time of death. 11:03 a.m. When they wheeled River back, we had prayed that he would pass quickly after life support was removed and that his little body wouldn't suffer. I secretly prayed that he would keep breathing on his own and shock the doctors and that they would wheel him back to us and say, "It's a miracle! He's breathing on his own! We can't explain it!" That didn't happen. We were told he breathed for four minutes and then took his last earthly breath. It was final. Our son was gone. And I wasn't allowed to be with him in those final moments.

We were then faced with the cruel reality of packing up our bags and going home. How does one do that? How does one just walk out the door of a hospital and go home with one less family member and piece of their heart? On the one hand, we didn't want to leave. I wanted to stay with Riv forever, but on the other hand we wanted to get home to London and Lincoln and get the terrible news over with. We had made the decision to keep the bigs at home during all of this. I don't know if it was the right thing to do, but we thought it best in our grief-stricken minds that they not witness their little brother seizing and hooked up to tons of machines. We wanted them to remember River happy and smiling and dancing as he was just days before, not lifeless and empty. They were so small, so young, so innocent. We didn't think they could fully process what was happening. And we didn't want to mess them up more than this horrific event probably already would. I can only pray as they grow up that they aren't angry with us for this decision. So far, so good.

Granger and I packed up our things. The staff tenderheartedly gave me little imprints of River's hands and feet, a lock of his red hair, and his heartbeat that had been recorded and saved on a flash drive. I had my son's heartbeat on a plastic flash drive. *What was happening?* We walked out of the hospital and across the parking lot to our car around noon. It was a pretty day, sunny and warm and bright. The blue, green, and white Donate Life flag was flowing in the breeze high atop the flagpole outside the hospital entrance. When a family chooses to give life to another, they fly the donor flag during the operation. As we glanced back at it one last time, Granger looked over at me crying and said, "I'm so sorry, baby. I don't think I will ever stop apologizing. I will say I'm sorry to you for the rest of my life."

As we made the mostly quiet drive home, I just put my hand on his leg and assured him that this could have happened to anyone and it wasn't his fault. The messy car seat full of half-eaten chips and sticky fruit snacks was empty of our baby. How would we break this news to the kids? We talked it over and said we would do what the hospital staff recommended. They encouraged us to be up-front and honest about it all. Not to sugarcoat anything or say River was in a better place or that he was sleeping. They said children are resilient and smarter than we give them credit for, and they advised us to just simply explain what had happened.

We pulled up to the house and came upon a smiling London and Lincoln in the drive. They looked so little and innocent running up to us with excitement, and we were about to break their hearts.

They had spent the past few hours drawing hearts all over the concrete with brightly colored sidewalk chalk. "Welcome home River" it said in shades of blue and red, yellow and green. As Granger and I slowly got out they excitedly asked, "Where's River?! Where is he, Mommy?"

"Come here guys, Mommy and Daddy have to talk to you."

London knew by our voices and faces that it wasn't good news. Granger scooped Lincoln up and we walked out back to a little space toward the woods. The four of us sat on the iron bench that faced the rubber tire full of dirt and tractors where River dug and played most days.

"Guys, when River fell in the pool, his brain went too long without oxygen . . . and bubby died. Our brains need oxygen to live, and when he fell in, he lost his oxygen and became very sick and couldn't survive." London instantly began to cry and Linc just stared blankly into the distance in the woods. We sat there holding each other, telling them any emotion they felt was okay and that we were there to talk about anything and answer any questions they had. We assured them that we would be okay. That we would make it through this together.

Because Lincoln was so young, he immediately went back to playing. We were kind of shocked by it, but as we've learned through all of this, all children process grief differently. He didn't fully release and cry until months later. London immediately ran inside and began grabbing all of River's things, making a shrine of sorts in her room to remember him. She grabbed his little tractors and favorite cars. She got his little dinosaurs and books and photos of him and set them all up on her shelves. The four of us slept together that night in our bed, holding each other tight, and got our first real night of sleep in three days.

I'll never forget opening my eyes for the first time that next morning when the sun began to peek through the shutters. For a second, I felt like it could have all been a dream. *Oh, please let it have been a dream.* But then, as my eyes adjusted to the light, the awful truth hit me: *River is dead. Our son is gone. His tiny body is lying in a cold morgue in Austin.* I quietly snuck out of the bed, careful not to wake anyone, put on my robe, and retreated to the back patio by the pool. Alone, in the dim light, I sat on the cement in front of the garage and screamed into his blanket as long and hard as I could. I began to sob uncontrollably.

My baby. I hate this. This isn't fair. Why didn't I put him to bed? Why didn't I take them inside? My baby needed me and I wasn't there. I wanted to take a stupid shower!

"Oh, River, I'm so sorry. I'm so sorry. You needed me," I sobbed. "I bet you were so scared. I'm so, so sorry."

The air was still and silent, and I prayed to the Lord to help me make it through this. To show me He was with me. Right at that moment a huge bird flew right over my head, almost scraping my hair as it did. The same thing had happened in the garden at the hospital one time when I asked God to help me to know River didn't suffer. I was praying by myself, and a large bird flew right over me. River's first word was *bird.* He always loved birds, planes, anything that could go fast or fly, and he would point them out in the sky. As I watched it glide, I stopped crying and marveled at the beauty of its wingspan and how it looked so free soaring across the clouds. I imagined River being just as free.

The weeks and months that followed were awful, as you can imagine. The house was quiet and dull. The harsh reality is that life doesn't stop for personal tragedies. The world keeps spinning. The sun still rises, time keeps ticking, responsibilities still need to be met, work still must get done. I hated doing all the mundane tasks like laundry and dishes. Everything felt pointless. I'm so grateful for the kindness and compassion of friends and family who rallied around us during that time. People brought meals, played with the kids, hung ribbons and flags all down our street. I really probably will never know all that everyone did as I was in such a fog for at least a month, but I am eternally grateful.

One evening, a friend of Granger's from the gym and his wife, a woman I'd never met, came by with food and a gift. She had spent weeks creating a prayer journal just for me. As I opened it, I wept at the beautiful prayers she had written, the delicate watercolor paintings, the scriptures she'd carefully selected, and even the pressed wildflowers she had placed between the pages—just like the ones River used to pick for me. This stranger's kindness, the way she poured love into every page, left a lasting mark on my heart. Needless to say, Naomi is now one of my dearest friends. She's a true prayer warrior and we have the sweetest friendship that I'll always treasure.

I'll never be able to repay the kindness that was shown to our family during that awful time. During a time of loss, decisions can be hard to make, yet you are forced to make so many all at once. Write an obituary, pick a funeral home and burial plot, choose burial clothes, pick songs. Still in a state of shock, I struggled to make even the smallest choices. Thankfully my sweet friends stepped in to help with our other children, helped with funeral arrangements and food, and even shopped for my funeral dress because I couldn't bring myself to do it.

No parent should be tasked with writing an obituary for a three-year-old and choosing clothes to bury their baby in, but I wasn't given a choice in the matter. He would be laid to rest barefoot, as he always was, and in a little Lightning McQueen tee and blue jeans. I bunched them up and brought them to my face, inhaling deeply, grasping for any remnant of his scent, kissed them, and drove to hand them over to the funeral director. Sitting in the funeral home flipping through the catalog of caskets about made me sick. Seventy-two hours ago, I was lifting my happy boy out of his high chair as he sang his "ABCDs," and then I was shopping for a box to bury him in. How was this real life? None of the caskets were right. They were all so polished and shiny. Not like Riv at all.

Riv was wild and undone. Messy and always covered in dirt. I settled on a shiny one made of cherry wood. I thought I could sand it and put wildflowers on it to make it more rustic. All of this felt so wrong. I left and cried as I got in the car with my friend Kelly. As we drove away, the funeral director called me and said he knew a guy who made custom caskets, that he could probably get a Lightning McQueen one made for us over the next week. This was another little glimmer of light during this time. Little things began to happen that could happen only by the grace of God. Things began to fall into place, showing me that I was being cared for. That Someone was looking out for me, for us. I wasn't alone. God saw me in my distress. He cared about me and my pain.

The Bible tells us in Psalm 34:18, "The LORD is near to the brokenhearted and saves the crushed in spirit."

Through all the pain I was enduring, I really did feel that the Lord was close. He showed up in the hospital, guiding our decisions and giving us a peace that didn't make sense; He showed up in the tenderness of the doctors and nurses in our time there; He showed up in the sweetness of our friends and family, in how they cared and provided for us, in the hundreds of sweet cards and gifts that were sent. Repeatedly, He showed His goodness by giving us strength when we had none to do really hard things.

June 11 came, and we were escorted by Georgetown PD in true River fashion, red and blue lights flashing and moving super fast to the service to honor River's life. It was beautiful. Over a thousand people came from all over to give tribute to our family. There were grade school and college friends in attendance, fellow artists from the music business, fans of The Smiths and Granger's music, and total strangers.

We had a Lightning McQueen car and Mater truck parked out front. We asked everyone to wear red, River's favorite color. My dress was simple and knee-length. Our friends had decorated the church stage with his toys and family photos, flowers, books, and his beloved cars and dinosaur plushies. I had originally wanted to speak to everyone in attendance, but when the time came and I stepped up to the microphone, my knees began to shake, I heard my childhood friend crying in the audience, I locked eyes with my neighbor (the one who came running over the night it happened), I saw London and Lincoln and our entire family so sad in the front row, and I just couldn't do it.

Granger took over and spoke beautifully about our sweet Riv. He told everyone we didn't want them to feel sorry for us, because we were given a special little boy for a time, and we were forever grateful for that. He told them that we trusted in this plan, we trusted in the Lord, and we were going to be okay. Words that we didn't fully trust or understand at that moment in time but words that God would come to fulfill in us soon after.

Paul, our close friend and editor of most of our YouTube, podcast, and music content, created the most beautiful video of River in all his silliness. I know it was so hard for him to do, and we are forever thankful. Everyone cried and laughed through all sixteen minutes of it. After hugging the lines of people offering their condolences, we headed off to the burial site. A light drizzle hit the windshield as we drove. Rain in Texas in June is unusual. Our summers are more known for droughts and triple-digit heat waves for weeks on end. Riv would be buried beside a gorgeous little old church that meant a lot to Granger's family. I felt peace for one of the first times since River's passing when we had visited out there and chosen the plot. It was beautiful and serene, overlooking the hills of Texas with the sunset and cows, his favorite animal, in the distance.

The hearse pulled up, and as I caught a glimpse of the red Lightning McQueen casket through the window, my throat felt like it would close up. My baby was inside about to be buried six feet below the earth. I hadn't been that close to him in five days. My heart pounded. I wanted to run over and rip the lid open and grab him and hold him, but I restrained myself, choking back tears. I don't think Lincoln fully comprehended that his little brother's body was inside as the ceremony started. He walked right up and put his little hands on the bright red casket, leaving a small, sweaty imprint on the top.

Our guitar player, Todd, began to play "Amazing Grace," and what was supposed to be just instrumental was suddenly interrupted as the pastor began singing the hymn loudly. It caught us all off guard, but it did add a little humor to this sad day. We released colored balloons into the sky, and everyone turned to the reception inside to eat. As we made our way toward the building, someone pointed out a tiny rainbow in the distance. It was small but it was there. A beautiful rainbow just River's size. A small gift in the summer heat of June—another reminder of the presence, promises, and closeness of God.

Funerals are strange. People are laughing and talking and eating fifty feet from a person being buried into the earth. I walked outside and began selecting yellow flowers from the top of the casket to keep and press, then just stood in the warm breeze kind of taking everything in. The funeral home had placed a little plastic placard in the ground at the burial spot with River's name and photo. I ran my fingers across his face in the picture. His sweet smile beaming. The photo of him taken while he was riding fast in the Ranger with his uncle Ty Ty, yelling for him to go faster, wind in his hair as they were being chased by a llama from our neighbor's yard. It felt like I was at someone else's funeral. *How could this be real?* My baby couldn't be gone.

But he was.

In their compassion, people kept trying to usher me back inside. They knew the grounds crew was about to lower him into his grave and the excavator would begin dumping dirt on top of him, and they probably didn't want me to witness it.

"It's okay." I smiled. "Riv loved excavators and dirt." But they still waited to do anything until I was back inside. As I entered, I looked out the window and could see the arm of the excavator beginning to dump the dirt into the hole. Granger later said how it was like a sick joke, watching River's favorite tractor—the one he played with every day on our dirt road, the one he begged to stop and watch every time we drove past a construction site—pouring dirt on top of him in the ground.

A little later, we all piled into the family Sprinter van and began our drive back home, entering our new reality as a family of four. I felt ill as we pulled away, leaving our little boy behind. The trek down the highway was quiet and somber. Everyone just stared out the window. I felt numb. How were we ever going to make it through this? Life would never be the same.

We hear the words *God is good* so often. People say "God is good" and others respond with "all the time." But this didn't feel good. This was some of the worst emotional, physical, and mental pain I had ever experienced. My body ached for my baby. My heart and stomach physically hurt. Over the next days and weeks I felt sick a lot. I cried so often on my bathroom floor, in my closet, shower, bathtub, and car. *If God is good and He loves us as the Bible says, why does He allow so much pain and suffering? Where is He in the midst of it?* These were all questions I wrestled with and began to unpack in the months that followed.

Grief is a painful process that challenges us to dig deep and confronts our beliefs at our innermost being.

If you are in a season of heartache or wilderness or waiting, it's okay to not understand yet. It's okay to be angry or sad or confused. Giving yourself permission to fully experience and express these emotions is crucial to healing. Grief is a painful process that challenges us to dig deep and confronts our beliefs at our innermost being. It doesn't follow a prescribed path to healing. There are books that talk about the five stages of grief (which can be helpful to read), but I've found it to be far less orderly. It's more like a tangled, jumbled mess. It's a complex, ongoing process that we learn to navigate over time. And everyone's journey is unique to their situation. No two trials are the same. So, we take it one breath, sometimes one heartbeat, at a time.

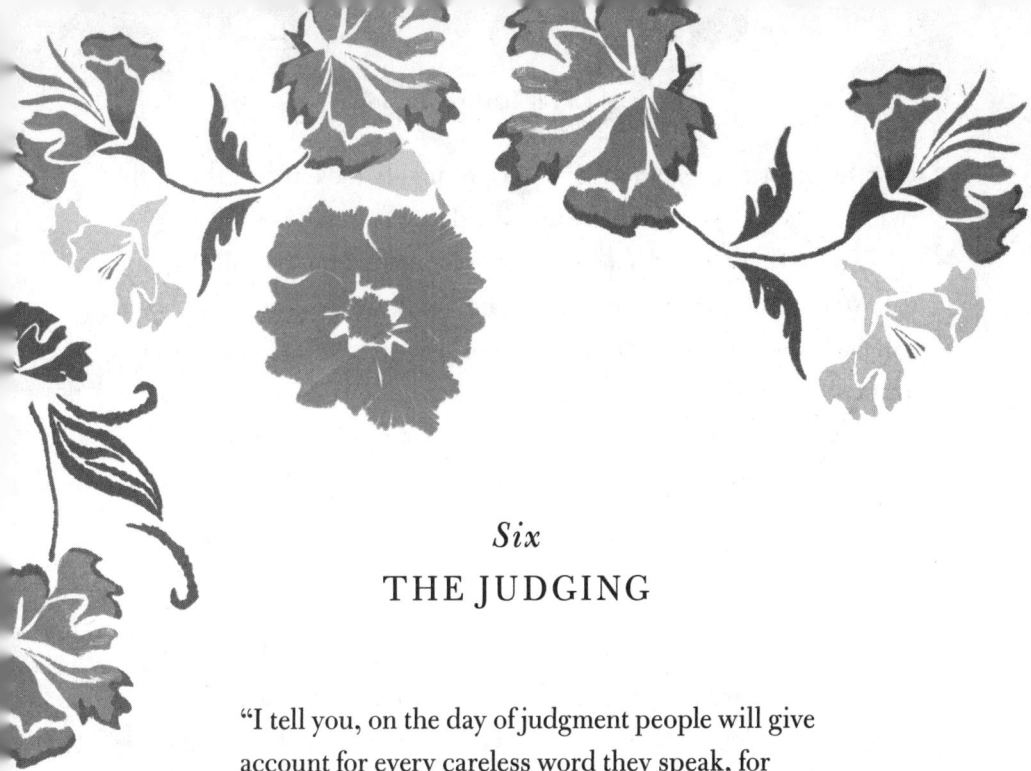

Six

THE JUDGING

"I tell you, on the day of judgment people will give
account for every careless word they speak, for
by your words you will be justified, and by your
words you will be condemned."

Matthew 12:36–37

In the days and weeks following our loss, the world outside seemed to collide with our personal tragedy. Because Granger was gaining recognition in the country music scene, news outlets quickly started reaching out to cover the story. We were approached by radio, print, and TV sources, all vying to be the first to break the news. But we wanted to be able to speak about our son honestly without any media putting their own spin on it for views or clicks. We decided to address our viewers and fans first, just as we had always done, on our family YouTube channel: The Smiths. We had started this channel just a few months prior to give Granger's fans an inside look at his life on the road versus my life at home with the kids.

Those first few videos were so fun to make. I cherish all the footage we have of our kids, especially now that River is no longer with us. We have so many adorable videos of Riv we can look back on, but at the time, we had a moment of thinking that maybe we should just take all our videos down and get off social media altogether. But then we thought, *This is real life. Terrible things happen, people die, and people all over the world are grieving something. Maybe we need to be open and honest and vulnerable in an attempt to help someone else who may also be grieving.*

I remember feeling incredibly nervous about speaking publicly even though it was just us and the camera in our backyard. My heart was heavy, and my eyes were swollen from sleepless nights and endless tears, so I did what I always did—I put on a little makeup. Not because I was trying to hide my pain but because it was a small thing that helped me feel somewhat normal in this inconceivable time. I've always loved makeup. I loved to play in it as a little girl. I would dig through my grandmother's and mother's makeup bags, dabbing rosy blushes on my cheeks and swiping cherry lip gloss across my lips, kissing the mirror as I danced around in my mom's clothes that were many sizes too big at my age. (This is something our daughter, London, does today; her current Sephora addiction is probably my fault.) It was a habit I'd kept with me as a new mom, a way to feel put together amid being covered in spit-up, leaked breast milk, and the chaos of motherhood. So, when it came time to film the video about River, I threw some on my face.

Two weeks after River passed, we went into the woods, to the spot where he used to play in the dirt with his cars and trucks, and we turned the camera on. It was hot and I was getting eaten by mosquitoes as the camera rolled. We talked about Riv and what had happened. We explained what we would do moving forward, both as a family and on our channel. We asked our viewers not to be sorry for us, thanked them for all their kindness and support, and then shared the same personal video we had shown to our family and friends at River's funeral. I tried to remain composed throughout the video, but as Granger reached to turn the camera off, the weight of everything came crashing down on me, and I lost it, breaking into tears in the backyard. You can see a split second of it before the video cuts off. We posted the video, and the comments started rolling in.

Ninety-nine percent of them were kind and caring, offering prayers and condolences. People shared their favorite memories of River, saying how much he had meant to them, how they had grown to love him through our videos. But that 1 percent—the harsh, judgmental comments—those are what gutted us and those were the ones we couldn't help but fixate on.

"Yeah, sure, she looks real sad with that face full of makeup."

"Look at her, she's smiling; you can tell she isn't that sad."

"Who puts on makeup after their child dies?"

As larger news outlets picked up the story, the criticism grew even more hurtful.

"A precious little boy drowned in a pool because his parents didn't watch him. Stop saying you're heartbroken because you obviously didn't care enough to keep an eye on him."

"Maybe you should have watched around the pool like a good mom."

"They should be in jail."

"If they weren't rich celebrities, they would have had their other kids taken away."

"Unfit parents. Lock them up."

"Is someone watching to make sure their other kids are supervised?"

"They had a kid and named him River and drowned him? Wow."

"She was probably on her phone. Idiot." (Ironic, because I couldn't even find my phone in that awful moment.)

I don't know what I was expecting, but the brutality of those comments hit me hard. I love my kids. I'm the mom who took all the proper vitamins three months before we planned to get pregnant. I didn't eat lunch meat, drink caffeine, or touch receipt paper during my pregnancies (sounds weird, but it's a thing). I nursed all of them for as long as I could. I worried about safe sleep. I was always two seconds behind them, telling them to get down off of things, to hold on tight, to be careful. I cut up their food really small, used organic sunscreen, put up gates and locks, and buckled them in car seats. I worried about screen time and too much sugar (something I have become very loose on since River died). I childproofed our home, locked up medicines, read all the books—and now strangers on the internet deemed me an unfit mother who had drowned her son.

Social media, which initially was meant to bring people closer, has done the opposite. Instead of uniting us in compassion, it's left most people even more isolated and lonely, viewing other people's lives through tiny screens with judgment and scrutiny. It's created faceless, cruel keyboard warriors who I am willing to bet would never dare to say what they type to a grieving mother's face. It's a dangerous place. And I really worry for those who don't have a good support system around them or stable mental health, because those awful words can drive someone to a point of no return.

In our deepest pain, the judgments and opinions of others can feel overwhelming.

In our deepest pain, the judgments and opinions of others can feel overwhelming.

I mentioned earlier how my mother-in-love lost her husband in 2014. They shared decades together, raising children, celebrating joys, weathering sorrows—lives beautifully intertwined. Losing him left an incredible ache in her heart, but she pressed on doing the only thing she knew how to do, which was put one foot in front of the other, trusting the Lord. For anyone who's lost a spouse or a loved one, you know this kind of grief—it's like a piece of your own soul has been torn away.

Sometime after his passing, she was out with family, trying to find moments of light and normalcy again. Out of the blue, a family member made the remark, "You know, people have been talking, and you seem a little too happy for someone who just lost their husband."

She was taken aback (as I am sure you were reading that), stunned that someone could say such a thing. Holding back tears but with quiet confidence, she responded, "Any joy you see in me is the joy of the Lord."

The Bible tells us, "The joy of the LORD is your strength" (Nehemiah 8:10).

Grief is not a one-size-fits-all journey, and no one should feel policed in their expressions of sorrow or joy. For those in pain, we already feel ashamed when we smile or laugh after a loved one passes. There is this sense of "How dare you laugh when you just buried your baby. What kind of person are you?" Some people may cry openly every day, while others hold back tears, appearing composed though they're breaking on the inside. Some grieve in silence, others in song or prayer, some in deep laughter as they remember special moments and memories.

Someone going through a trial, loss, or tragedy is already feeling so many incredibly difficult emotions; they don't need unsolicited advice about how they should perhaps be grieving differently. Because until you walk through pain yourself, you have no idea how you would respond.

Over time, I've learned to cling to the truth and to the people who truly know our hearts. We can't control what others say or think, and we shouldn't allow them to have access to those spaces

Grief is not a one-size-fits-all journey.

in our hearts and minds. We can only choose how we respond, just as Debbee did so beautifully. Granger always told me not to read the comments, but if I hadn't, I would have missed the kindness of so many and would have missed the opportunity to connect with others who were also walking painful paths like ours.

As time went on, the insensitive comments became less frequent, but they always resurfaced during milestones—when I posted a memory of River on his birthday or an anniversary. News stories would pick it up, and the hateful comments would start all over again. When I was younger, I always dreamed of being in magazines or on TV, but not like this. Not for this reason. I hated it. I hated that we were news. I never understood how people could say such awful things. But I tried to remind myself of the saying, "Hurt people hurt people." We read in Scripture that out of the heart the mouth speaks: "The good person out of the good treasure of his heart produces good, and the evil person out of his evil treasure produces evil, for out of the abundance of the heart his mouth speaks" (Luke 6:45).

When people type or say hurtful words, it's just an indication of the condition of their heart.

The comments used to make me spiral and be sad for days, but now I don't allow them to have that sting anymore. I don't allow them to take up residence in my heart and mind, and I often speak to our kids about how hurtful comments on social media can be truly harmful to others, so we always need to think about what we say or type. I remind them that our words carry weight, and as the Bible says, "The tongue is a fire, a world of unrighteousness. The tongue is set among our members, staining the whole body, setting on fire the entire course of life, and set on fire by hell" (James 3:6).

I genuinely pray for those who post such vile things. It shouldn't surprise us what people say when they are far from the Lord, and it's such a reminder that we are truly in a war. "For we do not wrestle against flesh and blood, but against the rulers, against the authorities, against the cosmic powers over this present darkness, against the spiritual forces of evil in the heavenly places" (Ephesians 6:12).

Sometimes the wounding words can come from well-meaning people. I don't know what words have been spoken over you in your pain, but I am sure they haven't always been pleasant. Perhaps they linger in your heart and resurface when you least expect it. Maybe you've heard comments like "A stronger person wouldn't let this destroy them," or "C'mon, you should be over it by now." Or perhaps if you're walking through the heartbreak of divorce, someone has insinuated that you're somehow to blame. If your marriage has suffered the betrayal of an affair, maybe you've felt the sting of whispers questioning if you could have done more to keep your spouse from stepping out. Or, like me, you've endured the unimaginable loss of a child, and the words "God needed them more than you" or "At least you still have two other children" have felt like a knife to your already shattered heart.

Whatever grief or judgment you're carrying, I want you to know you're not alone. Words can cut deeply, but they don't define who you are or the truth about a situation. Let this be a moment where you release the weight of those hurtful words to Him—the only one who truly knows the full story of your pain.

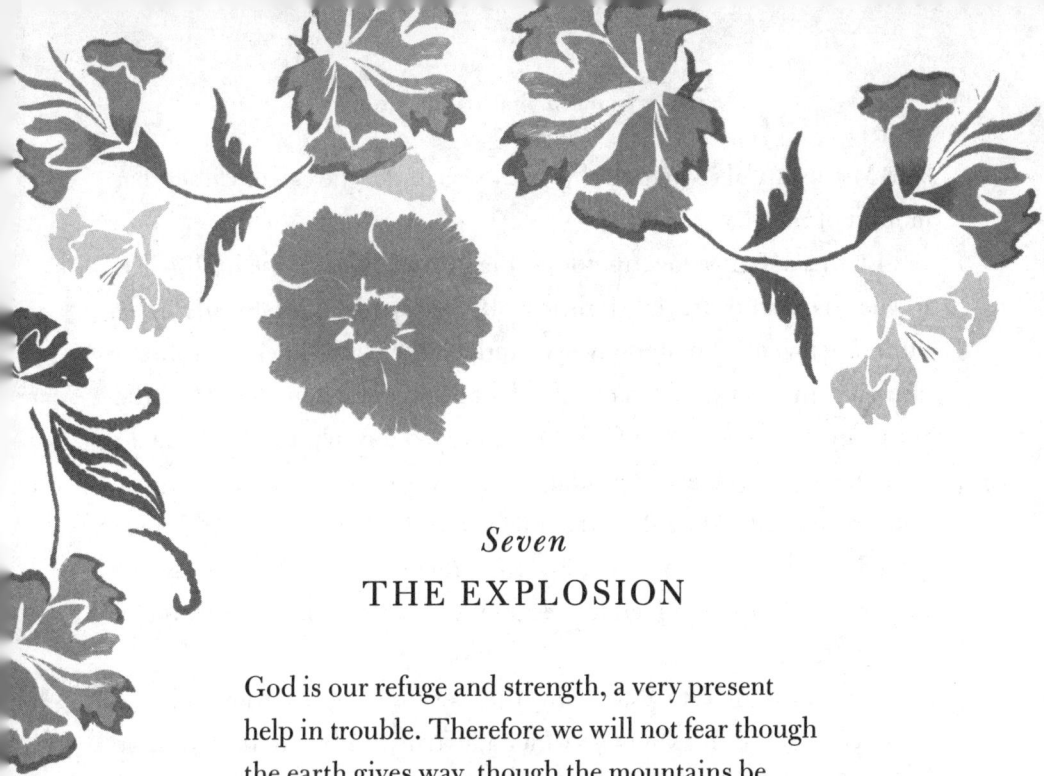

Seven

THE EXPLOSION

God is our refuge and strength, a very present
help in trouble. Therefore we will not fear though
the earth gives way, though the mountains be
moved into the heart of the sea, though its waters
roar and foam, though the mountains tremble at
its swelling.

Psalm 46:1–3

The week of July 4, the four of us went to Granger's parents' ranch to spend some time in the quiet of the Hill Country, near the church where River was buried. As everyone else posted photos of perfectly matched red, white, and blue attire, gearing up for Fourth of July parades and fireworks, my heart felt like it had been obliterated as I sat by the mound of rocks covering my son's grave. I walked up to his "angel spot" as we call it and felt as if I would hyperventilate. My heart raced; I took quick, shallow breaths; my shoulders began to shake. My son. My beautiful redhaired tiny baby was under the earth. Under that mound of rocks.

I laid a small yellow tractor on the grave and sat there in the dirt. I cried hard and prayed, fighting off the awful visions of his body buried below me. I closed my eyes and felt the wind. I heard the birds chirping and a lawn mower in the distance. I placed my hands on the rocks and prayed to God for peace; I prayed for help to know how to move forward, prayed for guidance for how to carry on and be a good wife and mother, though I was now just a shell of the woman I once was. Thankfully, as I prayed, my breathing began to slow, I was able to settle my heart, and I left feeling a sense of calm. Sadly, the next day wasn't the same.

Lincoln wanted to go with me the day after. I was hesitant to take him because I didn't know how much he truly understood. Again, he was only five. As we drove up to the church that next morning and walked inside, we talked about the old church and about Jesus. We prayed on our knees, the old wood floor creaking below us as sunlight pierced through the colorful stained glass windows. As we walked out, we signed the guest book, but instead of putting his own name, Lincoln signed it River. We exited the church and walked about fifty feet to Riv's spot. Linc stopped to grab his Froot Loops from the car and ran right up to the mound of rocks atop his little brother. He began playing with the cars and tractors that people had left behind at the service, rolling them all across the dirt.

"Where is River buried, Mama?" he asked softly.

I glanced down below his feet. "He's buried right there, sweetie."

Lincoln paused a few seconds, processing what I had said, and then with sudden, frantic urgency cried out, "We need him back, I wanna dig him up! Let's dig him up, Mama!"

"We can't, baby," I whispered as I held back tears.

"Why?! We need him! I want him back!" Simultaneously, he began picking up rocks off the top of the grave and throwing them.

"Baby, he's in heaven, he's not here." He didn't stop. He started to dig, his tiny hands grinding through the dirt, throwing rocks off the top by the handful. I grabbed him and held him tight and just cried. "Let's go back, sweetie. Let's go back to the ranch with Daddy and sissy."

"No! We need River, Mama! We need him!"

That may have been one of the saddest things I have witnessed to this day. My innocent five-year-old son crying, trying to dig up his dead little brother. His best friend in the world. *This isn't right. This isn't fair.* We did need River. This wasn't the way our lives were supposed to go. Why had God allowed this to happen? After a few minutes, I was able to get Linc settled and drove back to the ranch, but the whole way I was replaying what had just happened. I couldn't sleep that night.

The next morning, I told the family I needed to go home. I needed a little alone time. This was all too much. It had been over a month since I was alone, and I felt like I was about to explode. July 6, exactly one month after River took his last breath, was the first day I was able to release all my pent-up sadness and anger and confusion and pain. I pulled into our quiet house, and around 10 a.m. I walked upstairs to River's room, the room he and Lincoln shared, up to his now empty white crib, running my fingers over the little teeth marks still etched in the white wood. I sank down and screamed louder than I ever had; I cried the most guttural, animalistic cries on the floor. I threw things. I yelled, "I don't want pictures and memories and cards, I don't want blankets made of River's favorite T-shirts, I want my f***ing son!" If you had seen me, you would have probably locked me away in a strait-jacket. I was so broken. So sad that our son was taken from us. So angry that my family was forever changed. So confused as to how and why this had happened. I was seeking the Lord! I was going to church. I was drawing near to Jesus for the first time in my life. Why was this happening? I just couldn't make sense of any of it.

As much as I was hurting, I thank the Lord for the gift of lament. For the gift of tears. I mean, how incredible is it that in creating us, God gave us a way to grieve? A way to release our sorrow and grief by weeping. He doesn't expect politeness when faced with world-shattering pain. He invites us to lament and come to Him.

I love how the Scriptures show us so many stories of people who cried out to God in their pain. Job shaved his head and tore his clothes in anguish after losing everything he had and all his children. Hannah wept bitterly and prayed to the Lord in her barrenness, longing for a child. David refused to eat after his baby with Bathsheba became ill. Naomi was so grief-stricken after she lost her husband and both sons that she told her daughters-in-law to leave her and renamed herself Mara, meaning "bitter." We read of Mary and Martha devastated at the tomb of their brother Lazarus. When Jesus came, they cried to Him and said, "Lord, if you had been here, my brother would not have died" (John 11:21, 32).

He doesn't expect us to pretend away the hardest moments of our lives. Jesus Himself was brought to deep anguish when faced with the worst part of His own human journey. In His love, He has given us the ability to release all our frustrations and pain to Him. We don't have to carry it all. He invites us to come, to lay it at His feet. His Word says in Matthew 11:28–30, "Come to me, all you who are weary and burdened, and I will give you rest. Take my yoke upon you and learn from me, for I am gentle and humble in heart, and you will find rest for your souls. For my yoke is easy and my burden is light" (NIV). Thank you, Lord.

In our culture we have our worldly view of what we think *good* looks like. To us, good equals comfort. It equals ease, success, health, wealth, and pleasure. I myself had this view of good. I thought my life was good before all of this happened. Because before all of this, good to me was a loving marriage, healthy kids, a place we could call home, food and transportation for our family. To me good was happiness, no pain, no drama.

But our Lord, the Creator of all things, doesn't see good the way we do. His definition of good goes beyond our limited understanding. To God, good isn't just about what feels right or easy in the moment; it's about what shapes us into the image of His Son, what refines us, and what draws us closer to Him. Good to God is what fulfills His eternal purpose in our lives, even when it comes through great trials, unimaginable pain, and seasons or sorrow we would never choose. What we might see as unbearable, He sees as the very tool He uses to bring about His perfect plan for us. His good is always for His glory and our ultimate redemption.

Anytime I am overcome with sadness or pain or go back to my fleshly feelings that tell me none of this makes sense, anytime the Enemy tries to attack with lies, anytime someone's hurtful words pierce my heart, I look to the cross. Through the cross, I'm reminded that my pain, your pain, is not without purpose. The agony we feel on the bathroom floor, the days we question if we will ever feel whole again—Jesus understands it all. He's felt it all. He knows more suffering than any of us ever could. He endured betrayal, rejection, temptation, grief, hunger, thirst, false accusations, family tensions, beatings, and ultimately murder as He was nailed to the cross and felt the crushing weight of our sins. He felt the wrath of God that should have been poured out on us. He was forsaken so that none of His children would ever be.

You are not alone in your moments of feeling shattered, lost, or broken. In your pain, in your wilderness, in your waiting, God is present, right there with you in your lowest place, holding you in ways you cannot see. So if you find yourself on the bathroom floor, burdened by sorrow, confusion, anger, fear, or guilt, know this: You are not abandoned. God's love reaches deep into those broken places, and He invites you to bring every tear, every question, and every gaping wound to Him.

After a few days of being home from Fourth of July—the home

that was once so full of life, now somber, clean, and quiet—Granger and I came to the conclusion that we couldn't stay there any longer. It was an extremely hard decision to leave. I didn't want to move from that house and those woods. Those were River's woods where we explored, made forts, picked flowers, and turned over rocks to find bugs. Those were the woods where he tore in and out from around trees in his little John Deere tractor that his dad souped-up with a double-volt battery to make it run faster, and in a strange way, I felt as though I could still feel him there. But as the days dragged on, we realized we couldn't be the parents that London and Lincoln needed in that house. Every good memory was over-shadowed by the awful one we couldn't escape. The chlorinated aqua death trap outside still mocked us every time we pulled into the drive.

You are not alone in your moments of feeling shattered, lost, or broken.

Granger searched real estate apps every night for places we could move. By the grace of God, Granger's brother Tyler was selling his home just four miles away. It was grand and beautiful, way too large and extravagant for us, but it was a space filled with only good memories of Riv. The kids had played hide-and-seek all throughout that house. They had spent Christmas Eve the year prior playing games in matching red-and-white pj's and yelling "Ho, ho, ho!" into the night sky. It was a place the kids were familiar with, and it was available right away. We made the gut-wrenching decision to pack up and sell what we thought was our "forever home" and try to begin this new life that we were forced to start living with one less family member. Our home sold in eleven days.

Eight

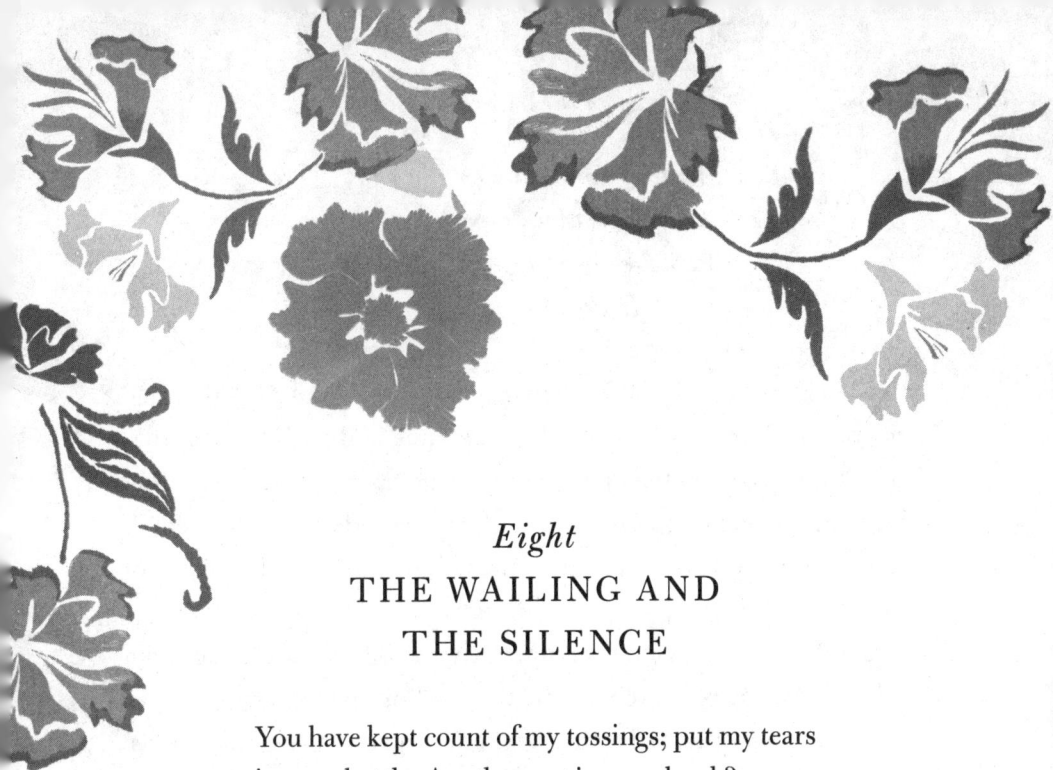

THE WAILING AND
THE SILENCE

You have kept count of my tossings; put my tears
in your bottle. Are they not in your book?
Psalm 56:8

We began packing every square inch of our life into plastic tubs and cardboard boxes just one month after our worst night as a family. I'll never forget the day I started taking down River's crib. With an Allen wrench in hand—the most frustrating tool for any assembly or disassembly—I made my way upstairs. I turned on some worship music, and the song "This Is a Move" began to play. I know this song is about much more than the move of a home, but the words hit me, and as the lyrics filled the room, I began to sob, twisting the tiny metal tool, unscrewing each piece of the crib, one by one. With every lyric crying out for God's presence and power to move, each slat of the crib fell, mirroring the tears streaming down my face.

Miracles happen when You move
Healing is coming in this room
Miracles happen when You move
Heaven is coming.[1]

When the last piece of the crib came down, I glanced at the time on my phone. It was 11:03 a.m., the exact time of River's final earthly breath. This was more than just a physical move; this, I was beginning to find out, was a move of the Spirit. A move we desperately needed. A move that would transform us in ways beyond a simple change of address.

As difficult as it was to take down River's crib, it wasn't that room that broke me. River rarely spent time in his room unless he was sleeping. The real heartache struck when I began to pack up the kids' playroom piece by piece. The playroom was upstairs, down the hall from their bedrooms, in a space where the ceiling came to a peak like an old attic. The carpet was soft and beige, a relic from the '70s—not at all aesthetically pleasing, but I'd kept it that way, knowing we'd be making plenty of messes up there. A large glass window adjacent to the door allowed us to watch the sunshine or rain, the trees, clouds, and birds.

The room was always a beautiful chaos: scattered with toys, a white play kitchen, books of all kinds, colorful posters, and a dark gray futon couch that the kids would leap from, pretending to be superheroes. There was a small dining table and chairs where we would color, sculpt with Play-Doh, or paint. This was the room where London, Lincoln, River, and I spent most of our days, pretending to be artists, doctors, or chefs, reading silly stories, wrestling, singing, and dancing. Now it was becoming empty and lifeless, just like I felt inside.

The house was ready for the next owners, and while the fresh paint and clean carpets made it appealing to anyone who would be coming in, to me it was sad and sterile. There were no more sticky Cheeto handprints on the walls, no more dinosaurs and cars lining the bathtub, no more superhero toothbrushes on the counter, no more paint splatters or glitter all over my laundry room where I let the kids create and make messes.

I cried so many tears alone in that empty house. It wasn't fair. I hated it—all of it. During the time of packing and the move, the kids began to act out more than usual. They always bickered as kids do, but they really began to fight and be mean to each other. I'm not normally an anxious person, but trying to be a good mom while navigating my own grief was one of the hardest roles I've played. Dealing with the absence of River and then having my two living children bicker and fight would raise my blood pressure, and I could feel my patience becoming thinner and my anxiety growing by the day.

I wanted to scream, "You are all you've got! Love each other! Be nice to each other!" I was angry. Angry that this had to happen. I was worried that this trauma was going to scar them for life. I tried to have patience and grace for them because I knew they were hurting, and they were so small. They didn't quite know how to express all they were feeling and at times took it out on each other. We decided to put them in play therapy with a local counselor in town around this time. After a few days of outbursts, London came to apologize one evening.

"I'm sorry, Mommy. I've just been mad since angel night."

My sweet girl. I grabbed her and pulled her close. "Me too, sweetie. I am so sorry that all this change is happening right now. I am so sorry that you are hurting and mad and that River isn't here with us anymore. I'm mad too. I wish I could make it all better right now, but I promise you, we will be okay. I love you, and Daddy and I are here for anything you need or anything you want to talk about."

The last thing I took down from the playroom was a two-by-four-foot black-and-white sign that read:

Be joyful in hope,
patient in affliction,
faithful in prayer.
Romans 12:12

When I bought that sign at Hobby Lobby a couple of years before, I liked the words, but they didn't carry the weight they do today. Looking back, I can see that God was guiding me, even then. I can see a lot of things looking back now. That sign still hangs on the wall in our bedroom today.

The World Keeps Spinning

When suffering strikes, it's nearly impossible not to look around and see the fragments of what your life used to be, scattered like debris after a storm. Everywhere you go, you're reminded of how things were—the life you had, the person you were before everything fell apart, the future that crumbled in your hands. Old places that once brought joy now feel like a punch to the gut. The park that used to echo with your little one's laughter as they slid down the slide now sits silent, the swings empty. The restaurant you once loved going to with your loved one is now just a painful reminder they are no longer here. Even everyday places like Target, where tantrums once tested my patience, now filled me with an aching longing for just one more meltdown over a Lightning McQueen car.

Each time we went for a Target run, River would take off running to the *Cars* section, climb up on the shelf, and pull down another "Li-Queen."

"I need this," he would say with his pointy-toothed River grin.

"Buddy, you have like ten of them already."

"Mama, I neeeeeed it."

THE WAILING AND THE SILENCE

I caved more often than not, but I am so glad I did. When River died, I was able to gift every person in our family their own bright red Lightning McQueen car. Many of those are carried around in vehicles and purses to this day.

The grocery store, school hallways, and especially your own home—all become reminders of what once was and what is no more. Some days, it was just too much to bear. I'd push through as long as I could, but there were times when I couldn't finish my shopping. I would pass by River's favorite snack or see another family walk by with a redheaded little boy, and it hurt too much. Some days I would leave my full cart in the middle of the store and just walk out.

I missed my old life. I missed my sweet boy. I missed the way things were. Life had never been perfect, but it was beautifully imperfect, and we were happy. Then everything was blown to shreds, and I was left standing in the wreckage, wondering how we were supposed to pick up the pieces.

I tried to get back to being the mom and woman I was, but that girl no longer existed. She died that day by the pool on June 4.

I cried myself to sleep more times than I can count, burying my face in River's blanket as I breathed in the now faint smell of him, longing for the last little bit of his scent. In the dimly lit room, if I squinted my eyes just right, the back of Lincoln's head looked like River's, and I would quietly cry as I was tickling his back, trying to envision that he was still with me. I hated myself for doing it. It made me feel guilty that I wasn't being present with Linc because I was trying to hold on to any glimpses of a child who was no longer here.

I drank more wine than I should have, trying to subdue the pain a little, but it only left me more agitated. Each morning felt like Groundhog Day as the weight of reality hit me all over again: *Eyes open, River is gone, and our lives are forever changed. I have to get up and do this all over again.*

Mornings were the hardest for me for a while. River and I used to snuggle on the couch while he drank his chocolate milk and I ran my fingers through his messy red hair. He would tell me about his dreams—usually about bears or dinosaurs. I just missed him so much. His laughter; his silly, sweet voice; his tantrums. I missed the way he'd line up his cars by color on the couch, wrapped in his soft blue blanket. I missed his kisses and the way he shook his hips as he played guitar and danced on the table to Granger's songs. I missed the way he'd grab my face and say, "I love you so much, Mama." I even missed the way he kept saying the word *butthole* constantly in the weeks before he died. I missed it all.

Some of the hardest days came when London and Lincoln went back to school that year. We had just moved into the new house, and although there were still boxes to unpack, the kids' rooms were all set up and ready. We wanted to give them as much normalcy as we could. Lincoln was starting kindergarten and London would be entering second grade. As August 15 rolled around, they excitedly dressed in their new clothes and grabbed their backpacks and lunch boxes, but as we walked out the door, reality set in that for the first time in seven years I was about to face the days alone.

Their school had a tradition of playing fun music during morning drop-off. Sometimes they even played some of Granger's songs, which the kids loved. The year prior, River, London, Lincoln, and I would dance and sing all the way to the big glass doors, River always leading the way, while London and Lincoln begged me to stop embarrassing them with my not-so-amazing dance moves. But this year, River was missing, and we didn't dance our way in like we used to. The familiar hallway felt longer and emptier without River's little feet running ahead, jumping over the cracks in the tile. It felt like all eyes were on us as we made our way down the hall.

We were no longer just the Smith family. We had become the family whose son drowned.

The Trauma Loop

As I walked back to the car, I could feel the emotion rising in me. I was alone. River should be with me. I wanted to collapse into the arms of our sweet friend Dena, the teacher and crosswalk guide who always greeted us with a smile and now looked at me with sad but helpless eyes. Somehow, I made it to the car before the tears came. I never once thought about ending my life during that time, but I will admit, I had these strange, intrusive thoughts—like a sudden urge to jerk the wheel off the road into a tree or drive off a tall bridge. They were hard to explain. It wasn't something I would have actually done. I didn't want to die. I needed to be there for my family. I *wanted* to be there for my family. I was just so angry, and the Enemy was relentless in making me feel like I had failed as a mother. *You should have put him to bed. You should have taken them inside. You should have scheduled swim lessons sooner. This is all your fault. You didn't protect him.*

I wept almost every day on the drive back to our empty, quiet house. The absence of River filled every corner. He was everywhere and nowhere all at once. I missed everything about him, and I couldn't see how we would ever move forward. Yet, somehow, life kept spinning around us and we managed to put one foot in front of the other. Granger had gotten back on the road rather quickly for work, partly because he had twelve guys on salary who depended on him, partly because the distraction of staying busy helped him keep his mind off the pain. We joined him on the first tour back, trying to make life feel as normal as possible for the kids. But it was all for show. I could tell Granger didn't enjoy the stage anymore. He couldn't wait for the last song to be over so he could retreat to the bus to be with us. As the months went on, I had the sense that he wouldn't be doing music like this much longer.

After River died, everything I once enjoyed felt meaningless. I used to unwind with cheesy TV shows like *The Real Housewives*. I'd joke that since my life had no real drama, I liked to watch it on TV. But after losing him, that kind of noise became unbearable. The shows that once entertained me now felt like empty trash. I see now that they always were.

Everyday conversations felt equally intolerable at times. People would complain about things that now seemed so trivial and stupid, and I'd have to fight the urge to scream. It wasn't their fault—they hadn't experienced the kind of trauma I had—but it was hard to reenter the world after everything that had happened and talk about petty, superficial things. It made me think of others in my life who had gone through seasons of suffering and the dumb things I probably talked about during that time that perhaps made them want to punch a hole through some drywall.

The worst part was the haunting visions that replayed in my mind like a broken record. I couldn't escape the memories of that night. I saw Granger's terrified eyes and River's swollen, purple face, his eyes rolled back in his head. I could hear the sounds of CPR, feel my hands pressing on his tiny chest. I was covered in vomit, and my beautiful baby boy was dead on the concrete. These images and sounds ambushed me relentlessly, often in the middle of normal conversations or in my dreams, and they were usually the first thing that assaulted my mind when I woke up each morning.

We called it "the slideshow"—a cruel mental replay of the trauma, as if my brain was trying to make sense of it all. Well-meaning people told me it was "okay to be depressed" and suggested I take medication like Xanax to cope. I knew some people needed those medications, especially after something so traumatic, but I resisted. Yes, I was broken, but I didn't want to mask the pain. I was afraid that if I didn't face it head-on, it would only return later, stronger, and with a vengeance.

I tried hard to feel normal again. But I just couldn't. I forced myself to go out to dinner, to sit with my friends and chat like I used to. As they talked, their words seemed distant, almost foggy. How could I focus on small talk when visions of my dead child flooded my mind? The contrast between their lighthearted conversations and the dark images in my head was extreme. More than once, I had to just get up and leave the table. Thankfully, I had a circle of friends who understood. They didn't ask questions or make me feel guilty for leaving. Often, they'd quietly follow me out, just to make sure I was okay.

One night, I pushed myself to go to my best friend's birthday party. This is the same friend who flew in from out of the country to be with me in the hospital the night River drowned. She had always been there for me, celebrating the important moments in my life, and I wanted to do the same for her. I told myself I could handle it. *Just a couple of hours to show my support. You've got this, Amber.* But as I stood there, watching everyone else drink, dance, laugh, and play games, it felt insufferable. The joy in the room was like a spotlight on my pain, reminding me that I didn't feel joy anymore. I didn't feel much of anything. I couldn't pretend. I couldn't force myself to join in. I found her in the crowd, and she could tell by my eyes I was leaving. I hugged her tightly and told her how much I loved her. I apologized, choking back tears, and said, "I'm so sorry, I just can't do it. Not yet, anyway."

If you're reading this and you're in that place—the place where the world has moved on but you feel like you're frozen in time—I see you. I remember sitting at those tables, trying so hard to be "normal," to laugh, to participate, but feeling like an outsider to my own life. You're physically there but mentally on another planet. And no one seems to fully understand the depth of the darkness inside you.

To anyone who finds themselves in this space, I want you to know that you don't have to force yourself to "keep up" with others. There is no "right" way to grieve and no time frame that anyone else can set for you. You are allowed to step away when you need to, to leave the party early, to say no to something, to have those moments where you just can't hold it together. Grief is isolating enough without the added weight of feeling like you need to explain or justify your pain. You don't.

I wish I could sit with you in the silence of those moments, just to be present and bear witness to what you're going through. Not to fix it—because really hard things can't be fixed—but to simply sit beside you in the sorrow, in the weeping, and in the silence. I wish I would have been better at that before my loss. I failed my friends and family before living it myself.

Allow yourself the grace to feel exactly as you do.

The Bible tells us that the Holy Spirit intercedes for us with groanings too deep for words (Romans 8:26–27). In the unspeakable pain, God Himself sits with you, holding the pieces you can't even lift, praying the prayers you can't even pray.

If you're struggling to find joy, if you feel like you don't belong in the "normal" world right now, that's okay. Allow yourself the grace to feel exactly as you do. The Bible says there is a time for everything:

> For everything there is a season, and a time for every
> matter under heaven:
> a time to be born, and a time to die;
> a time to plant, and a time to pluck up what is planted;
> a time to kill, and a time to heal;
> a time to break down, and a time to build up;
> a time to weep, and a time to laugh;
> a time to mourn, and a time to dance.
> (Ecclesiastes 3:1–4)

This place you're in is holy ground, and you can feel all of it, right where you are. If whatever you are facing is new and fresh, allow yourself to feel it all. Wrestle with it. There is no rush to leave it just yet. The God who holds every tear is with you, and He is working, even here.

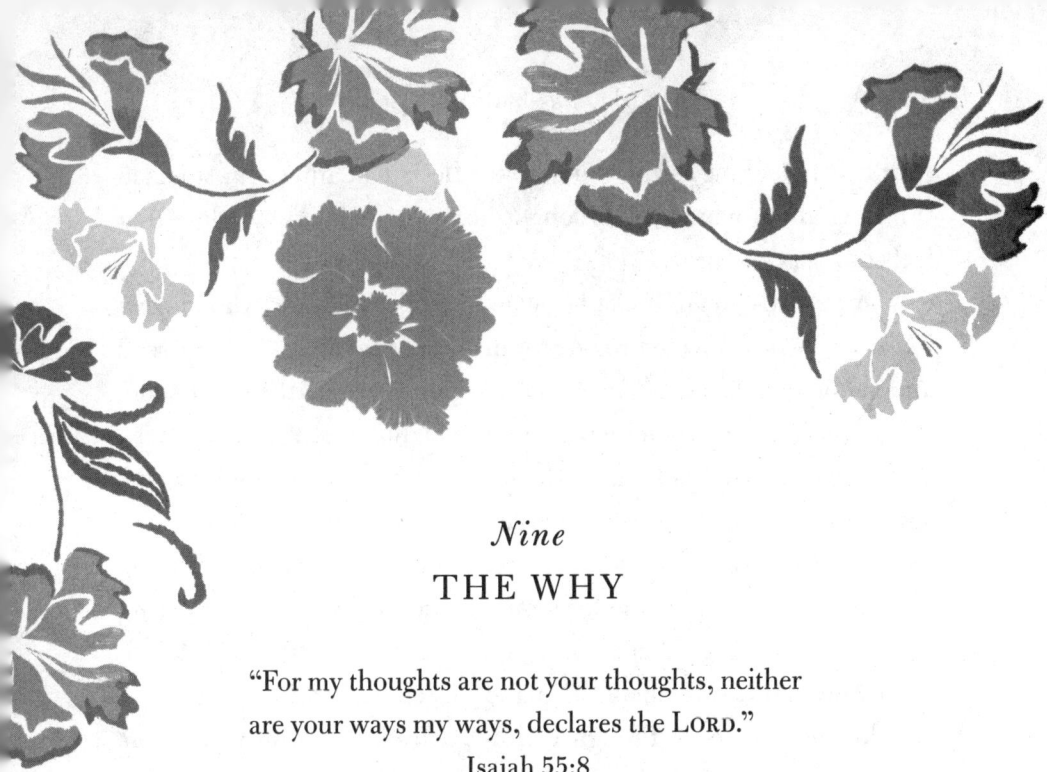

Nine

THE WHY

"For my thoughts are not your thoughts, neither
are your ways my ways, declares the LORD."
Isaiah 55:8

What do you do when your life gets flipped upside down? When nothing
is as it should be? When someone or something is ripped from you in
seconds? One of the most-asked questions about God on Google is
"Why does God allow suffering and evil?" Haven't we all thought this
at one point in our lives? The question becomes even more real when
tragedy and heartache hit us personally.

For some of you, the grief feels like it will swallow you whole, and
you find yourself, like me, crying on the bathroom floor, the weight
of it all pressing you down, feeling all-consuming. Maybe you're there
right now, tears streaming down your face, hands clenched on the cold
tile, wondering how you'll ever get up. Maybe you're the mother who
just received the devastating news that there is no longer a heartbeat,

your heart breaking as you slump to the floor, clutching your stomach thinking about what will no longer be, overwhelmed by a loss that feels too heavy to bear.

Or perhaps you're the father who feels like a failure, who lost his job and can't see how to provide for his family anymore, embarrassed and sobbing in secret because you're supposed to be the strong one, the leader. Or maybe you're the son or daughter weeping as you take that hit of methamphetamine, the one you swore you wouldn't take again; you hate yourself for it, but the grip of addiction has its claws in too deep. You may have just discovered your spouse has been cheating on you, living a double life for months, and now you are wondering how you will take another step.

In my darkest moments, I made myself search for the light. I sought the Lord even though I didn't truly know Him yet. It was in the rawness of my grief that I began to see more clearly the One who does know our pain intimately. I came to know Jesus not as a distant figure but as one who suffers and cries with us, who wept at the tomb of His friend Lazarus not just because He loved him but because He hates the effects of what sin and death have done to this world. I saw Him as the One who truly understands the depth of our sin and sorrow because He bore it Himself on the cross. Now, five years down this road of heartache, I find myself agreeing with the words of one of my favorite suffering women, Elisabeth Elliot, who said, "I've come to see that it's through the deepest suffering that God has taught me the deepest lessons. And if we'll trust Him for it, we can come through to the unshakeable assurance that He's in charge. He has a loving purpose. And He can transform something terrible into something wonderful. Suffering is never for nothing."[1]

These words have become a lifeline for me, reminding me that even in the depths of my despair, God is moving. It doesn't make the pain less real, but it gives it a purpose—a purpose that I now see unfolding in ways I could never have imagined.

If I could, I'd like to take you back to the story of Lazarus. The Scriptures say that when word came that Lazarus was sick, Jesus responded, "This illness does not lead to death. It is for the glory of God, so that the Son of God may be glorified through it" (John 11:4). Scripture continues, "Now Jesus loved Martha and her sister and Lazarus. So, when he heard that Lazarus was ill, he stayed two days longer in the place where he was" (vv. 5–6).

I'm sorry, what? Jesus heard Lazarus was sick. He loved him and his sisters, yet He stayed where He was and waited two more days before coming. Why?

We go on to read the purpose. Jesus told His disciples,

> "Our friend Lazarus has fallen asleep, but I go to awaken him." The disciples said to him, "Lord, if he has fallen asleep, he will recover." Now Jesus had spoken of his death, but they thought that he meant taking rest in sleep. Then Jesus told them plainly, "Lazarus has died, and for your sake I am glad that I was not there, so that you may believe. But let us go to him." (vv. 11–15)

The purpose of the waiting was so that they would believe. For their sake, out of love, He waited. It was thought back then that the spirit of a person would hover over a body for a few days, so Jesus waited so they would know for sure that what He was about to do could be done only by God and would result in belief in His name.

When Jesus arrived at the tomb, Lazarus had been dead four days.

> Martha said to Jesus, "Lord, if you had been here, my brother would not have died. But even now I know that whatever you ask from God, God will give you." Jesus said to her, "Your brother will rise again." Martha said to him, "I know that he will rise again in the resurrection on the last day." Jesus said to her, "I am the resurrection and the life. Whoever believes in me, though he die, yet shall he live, and

everyone who lives and believes in me shall never die. Do you believe this?" She said to him, "Yes, Lord; I believe that you are the Christ, the Son of God, who is coming into the world." (vv. 21–27)

Martha then called to Mary to come, and she, too, cried to the Lord and said if He would have been there Lazarus wouldn't have died. When Jesus saw her weeping, the Scriptures say Jesus was deeply moved and greatly troubled. It says, "Jesus wept" (v. 35). The story continues:

Then Jesus, deeply moved again, came to the tomb. It was a cave, and a stone lay against it. Jesus said, "Take away the stone." Martha, the sister of the dead man, said to him, "Lord, by this time there will be an odor, for he has been dead four days." Jesus said to her, "Did I not tell you that if you believed you would see the glory of God?" So they took away the stone. And Jesus lifted up his eyes and said, "Father, I thank you that you have heard me. I knew that you always hear me, but I said this on account of the people stand-ing around, that they may believe that you sent me." When he had said these things, he cried out with a loud voice, "Lazarus, come out." The man who had died came out, his hands and feet bound with linen strips, and his face wrapped with a cloth. Jesus said to them, "Unbind him, and let him go." (vv. 38–44)

I've been unpacking these verses in a Bible study I've been doing with some friends, and verses 5–6 in particular hit me: "Now Jesus loved Martha and her sister and Lazarus. So, when he heard that Lazarus was ill, he stayed two days longer in the place where he was." *Because* He loved them, He waited. He could have gone and caused Lazarus to get well or stopped his death in some way, but He waited so that they would believe and have eternal life in Him.

Jesus could have saved River. He could have brought him back to us and we would have had a good story to tell, but for exact reasons I don't know, He didn't. But I do know He saw the ultimate outcome of our pain and what it would produce in us—belief and trust in Him.

Often we can think that Jesus isn't coming through for us, but we must remember that He sees the larger picture. He saw the ripple effect of belief that would take place when He miraculously brought a dead man back to life with a word. Death doesn't have the final say, Jesus does, and when we believe and trust in Him, we, too, shall never die. Jesus has authority over death.

To those of you who are currently in the midst of your own pain, wrestling with the agonizing question of why and wondering where God is, I want to remind you that you have someone who meets you in your lowest points of pain, who weeps with you over the fallen nature of this world, but who also holds the keys to death and the grave. Who calls dead bodies to life in Him. Who offers abundant life not only eternally but right now. And who loves you so much that He may wait, or allow a tragic season in your life, in order to bring you to saving faith in Him.

Only by turning to Jesus was I given peace. I wasn't given answers to all my questions, but I was given His presence, His love, His Word, and His comfort. And that has been enough to sustain me.

Your tears are seen, your pain is known, and your suffering is never for nothing.

Whether you're crying on the bathroom floor because of a devastating diagnosis, a broken relationship, or the loss of a child, know that Jesus weeps with you in your pain. He goes before you and is faithful to lead you through it, transforming something terrible into something wonderful. Your tears are seen, your pain is known, and your suffering is never for nothing.

When my world and everything I knew shattered around me, I was desperate—desperate for any flicker of hope, any ray of light that could pierce through the overwhelming darkness that enveloped me.

I craved stories of others who had suffered the unimaginable loss of a child. How did they survive? Did they ever find joy again? What did they do when their hearts were breaking, when every day felt impossible? I scoured bookstores and the internet, searching for every book on hope, heaven, and loss that I could find. There weren't many on drowning, but I devoured the few that existed, along with countless others on heartache and grief. There's something so comforting, something deeply intimate, in knowing that someone else has walked the same painful path, even if the details differ. I longed to hear from those who had navigated these treacherous waters before me.

As I read their stories and began to immerse myself in devotionals, I started to feel a glimmer of hope. If they could do it, maybe I could too. Maybe, just maybe, we could be okay. Not today, but someday. Perhaps it wouldn't hurt this much for the rest of our lives. These people weren't pretending it was easy—in fact, I admired their brutal honesty about the pain. It made me feel like I wasn't crazy. But they were still moving forward, still putting one foot in front of the other. They had found a way to keep living, to keep loving, even after their world had been turned upside down. And that's what I knew I had to do too.

The more I read, the more I began to realize in vivid detail that suffering is all around us and always has been. I became drawn to stories of suffering, particularly the stories of women. Their grit, their courage, their fortitude in the face of agonizing pain ignited something within me. I wanted to be one of those women. I wanted to be a woman who suffered well. I wanted to show others that there is hope, even on your darkest days.

Women like the aforementioned evangelist and missionary Elisabeth Elliot, whose husband Jim was killed in Ecuador by the spears of Auca tribesmen in 1956. Can you believe she actually went back with her small daughter to live with the very men who had killed her husband? Would you be able to do that? Through her bravery, forgiveness, and love, she helped lead them to Jesus. In response to the tribe's new faith, the people renamed themselves Waorani (meaning "they are true people"), changing from their former name Auca, which means "savage." You'd think that losing Jim would have been enough suffering for a lifetime, but she later lost her second husband to cancer and eventually passed away in 2015 after a hard battle with dementia.

Or consider another woman, not quite as well-known, Annie Johnson Flint. She lost both parents at an early age and grew up in an adoptive family that, by the grace of God, taught her the Scriptures. In her early twenties, Annie developed a painful arthritis that eventually left her hands disfigured and rendered her unable to walk, bound to a wheelchair. The pain was so severe that she could rarely sleep. Yet, with her eyes on Christ, Annie became a poet, writing about God's goodness. Can you picture it? This woman, with crippled, aching hands, bound by suffering, wrote some of the most beautiful truths about the goodness of our God:

God hasn't promised us an easy life free from pain and trials, but He has promised us His presence.

> God hath not promised smooth roads and wide,
> Swift, easy travel, needing no guide;
> Never a mountain rocky and steep,
> Never a river turbid and deep.
> But God hath promised strength for the day,
> Rest for the labor, light for the way,
> Grace for the trials, help from above,
> Unfailing sympathy, undying love.[2]

Wow.

God hasn't promised us an easy life free from pain and trials, but He has promised us His presence. He has promised us just enough strength for the day. He has promised us light in the dark and unfailing love.

"Fear not, for I am with you; be not dismayed, for I am your God; I will strengthen you, I will help you, I will uphold you with my righteous right hand."
Isaiah 41:10

It is the LORD who goes before you. He will be with you; he will not leave you or forsake you. Do not fear or be dismayed.
Deuteronomy 31:8

Even though I walk through the valley of the shadow of death, I will fear no evil, for you are with me; your rod and your staff, they comfort me.
Psalm 23:4

But he said to me, "My grace is sufficient for you, for my power is made perfect in weakness." Therefore I will boast all the more gladly of my weaknesses, so that the power of Christ may rest upon me.
2 Corinthians 12:9

Again Jesus spoke to them, saying, "I am the light of the world. Whoever follows me will not walk in darkness, but will have the light of life."
John 8:12

Your word is a lamp to my feet and a light to my path.
Psalm 119:105

Annie didn't become cynical, angry, or bitter, though she had every reason to. She kept her eyes on eternity and God's steadfast love, even through adversity, and penned some of the most beautiful words about her Savior:

He giveth more grace as our burdens grow greater,
He sendeth more strength as our labors increase;
To added afflictions He addeth His mercy,
To multiplied trials He multiplies peace.
When we have exhausted our store of endurance,
When our strength has failed ere the day is
     half done,
When we reach the end of our hoarded resources
Our Father's full giving is only begun.
Fear not that thy need shall exceed His provision,
Our God ever yearns His resources to share;
Lean hard on the arm everlasting, availing;
The Father both thee and thy load will upbear.
His love has no limits, His grace has no measure,
His power no boundary known unto men;
For out of His infinite riches in Jesus
He giveth, and giveth, and giveth again.[3]

Sweet friend, suffering is sadly unavoidable. But misery is optional. If you haven't experienced some form of suffering yet, you will. It crosses all boundaries—age, nationality, social status. It doesn't care about your wealth, your background, your follower count on social media, how faithful you are, or whether you've been through it many times before. Suffering is a universal experience, indiscriminate in its reach. So, the question becomes this: What will we do with it? Will we let it destroy us and make us bitter, or will we allow it to catapult us deep into the arms of Christ, the only one who can truly heal our hearts and show us how to grow from it?

When we face suffering, heartache, or disappointment, we have a choice in how we respond. We can turn away from God, angry and jaded, letting the pain harden our hearts. Or we can fall to our knees, surrendering our hurt to Him, and trust that He is still good, even in the pit of our darkest days. We can seek the comfort and solace that only He can provide.

The stories I read gave me glimpses of hope—tiny sparks that maybe, just maybe, this wouldn't ruin me. And as I began to walk through my own grief with newfound peace and even moments of joy, I felt a deep desire to share that with others. I want you to know that there is purpose in your pain, that there is hope even when it feels like the light has gone out. Your story is not over, and the most devastating thing that has happened to you is not the end. Death and pain do not get the final say.

When my kids are hurt or sad, they come running to me. I scoop them up in my arms, wipe away their tears, and hold them close. I comfort them, whispering words of encouragement and love, embracing them until they feel safe again. One of the sweetest acts of tenderness is to wipe away someone's tears. Yet, with my children, the tears often return—the next skinned knee, the next harsh word from a friend at school, or the next disappointment. But our good God, our Savior, promises something far greater. He promises that one day, He Himself will wipe away every tear—not just once, but forever. For all eternity. And until then, He holds us in the depths.

Stories have the power to change lives. When people take their brokenness and use it for the glory of God, to help others, it creates a ripple effect that can shift generations. The stories of those who have walked through trials and perhaps even found treasures in their suffering help to encourage and prepare those who will walk that path after them. By sharing our stories, we help to light the way for others, showing them that even in the darkest night, they are not alone and there is still hope. As Bible teacher and speaker Kristi McLelland said, "Generations are impacted when a woman lives with hope in her hands."[4] I want our story and how we walked through this loss to

Stories have the power to change lives.

be one of the hundreds of thousands of stories among other suffering saints lighting the way home and pointing people to our sovereign, gracious God.

I've used that word *sovereign* a few times throughout this book. You may be wondering what it means. Sovereignty as it relates to God describes His ultimate authority, power, rule, and control over all of His creation. It means that He is holding everything together and orchestrating all things according to His good and perfect will. It means nothing happens outside of His control, and His plans cannot be thwarted. His sovereignty assures us that even in our deepest pain, even when everything feels out of control, He remains steadfast.

Holy Ground in the Valley

I knew I couldn't stay in that place of pain forever. My other two children needed their mom, and not an angry, distant version of her. They were grieving, too, and they deserved a normal childhood filled with joy, not trauma. Granger was carrying his own guilt and shame, and I needed to be there for him as well. I had to find hope. I turned up worship music all day long, singing through tears. I pored over devotionals, searching for any glimpse of encouragement and light. I kept reading books on suffering.

I dragged myself to church each Sunday, sobbing through every song, begging God to meet me in my despair. It would have been so much easier to give up, to stay in bed and cry all day. But what good would that have done? What good would that have been for my family, for River's legacy? I needed to fight for the hope and healing that somehow, deep down, I knew only Jesus could give. I wasn't there yet, but I was searching, reaching for any hint of His light in the darkness.

I don't know why some people run to God in their pain whereas others turn and run the other direction, but I do know this: God was drawing me in. I see now how He had been drawing me in for the year leading up to River's passing. Up to that point Granger and I would have said we knew Jesus, but we weren't living for Him. We had no real fruit of a saving faith in Christ, but after that cancer scare with River in 2017, I felt the pull to take the kids to church. I felt that we needed to begin giving them a foundation of faith. I started to read devotionals and books for moms seeking quiet time with Jesus. I attended Christian women's conferences and joined my first Bible study. I was still very new to this Christian thing, but I was beginning to feel like we were on the right path, and I was feeling real peace in my life for the first time.

I'd gather with the ladies one night a week and we would share delicious homemade food, then pray over one another and dive into the Word together.

I was new to the Bible, so I felt like I was playing catch-up. I remember sitting there, searching the table of contents to find where a certain book was, while the other ladies could turn right to a specific passage without a second thought. But they never made me feel behind. I was always encouraged, supported, and loved by these women. They challenged me in my faith, they prayed with me, and they walked alongside me when my world came crashing down. Those "Jesus Girls" were there, helping to hold me up when I didn't have the strength to stand on my own.

Looking back with fresh eyes, I see now how the Lord was gently preparing me for what was coming. In His loving provision, He was imprinting Scripture on my heart and surrounding me with a community of women who would walk with me through the hardest days of my life. God knew I would need them. He knew I couldn't walk that road alone.

John Piper, one of my favorite pastors and theologians, said, "God is always doing 10,000 things in your life, and you are aware of about 3 of them."[5] I didn't know it at the time, but God was working behind the scenes, placing people in my path for the very moment I would need them most. Perhaps He is doing that for you right now.

We were never meant to walk through life alone. From the very beginning, God created us for community. Genesis 2:18 says, "It is not good that the man should be alone." We are created to be in relationship—not just with God but with one another. Yet, when suffering hits, so often we try to go it alone. We retreat, pull back, and isolate ourselves, in shame or guilt or fear, thinking we

We were never meant to walk through life alone.

need to bear our burdens by ourselves. But that's exactly what the Enemy wants. Isolation is his playground. When we're alone, we're more vulnerable and open to his lies, to the voice in our heads telling us we're too broken, too far gone, or that no one else understands our pain.

If you've ever had a child bring you flowers they've picked, you know they wither and die if you don't immediately get them in water. And even then, because they are no longer connected to the source, they don't last long. The Bible reminds us that Jesus is our true Vine. Our true source of hope, life, healing, and peace.

> "I am the true vine, and my Father is the vinedresser. . . . Abide in me, and I in you. As the branch cannot bear fruit by itself, unless it abides in the vine, neither can you, unless you abide in me. I am the vine; you are the branches. Whoever abides in me and I in him, he it is that bears much fruit, for apart from me you can do nothing." (John 15:1, 4–5)

When we isolate ourselves in suffering, we miss out on one of the very things God has given us for healing. The Enemy wants to trap you in misery and keep you broken and alone. He knows you can do nothing apart from the Lord. He knows if he can keep you alone, you can't bear fruit. But God calls us to come together, to encourage one another, and to bear each other's burdens. It's a picture of what community is meant to be—a place where we can weep together, rejoice together, and walk through the highs and lows of life, hand in hand. So, I chose not to be isolated in my hurt. I made myself go to groups and studies and church even when I wasn't feeling up for it. Many times we have to make ourselves do the things we don't want to do, and the feelings will follow.

After River's death, my friend Allison suggested I attend a GriefShare class near me. It was a thirteen-week course with videos and a workbook walking you through whatever hardship you were navigating, and even though I didn't know if I was ready, I made the choice to show up. I'm so thankful I did. The women I met there became some of the greatest blessings in my life. Our leader, Suzanne, is like an angel walking on earth. She opened her home to us, night after night, leading us through grief, prayer, and the Word. She reminded us every day of who we are and whose we are—God's beloved children. Suzanne had her own stories of loss—losing her mother to pancreatic cancer and her little sister to suicide—along with being betrayed by a colleague in business. And yet, through all her suffering, she kept her eyes on Jesus and allowed the Lord to use her as His instrument to bring others to Him.

When we isolate ourselves in suffering, we miss out on one of the very things God has given us for healing.

She didn't let her grief turn her inward or isolate her. Instead, she let God use it to create a community of healing for other women. She started a group called GiG (Growing in Grace), in honor of her dear friend Bobbie who battled and later passed away from her fight with ALS, formerly known as Lou Gehrig's disease. Through all her loss, she has kept saying, "I just want to be His vessel, to be Jesus with skin on." She has led countless women through their pain, pointing them back to the one true Healer: Jesus. Her story is a testament to the power of community—how God uses the people around us to be His hands and feet in our moments of deepest sorrow.

Suz is now seventy-five years young, dealing with her own health struggles day to day, yet still opens her home multiple times a week, gifts prayer beads and shawls to those who grieve, and encourages so many by living out her faith for the world to see.

In your hard times you are going to need the love and care of other brothers and sisters in Christ. Hebrews 10:24–25 urges us, "And let us consider how to stir up one another to love and good works, not neglecting to meet together, as is the habit of some, but encouraging one another, and all the more as you see the Day drawing near." God designed us to be in community. Ecclesiastes 4:9–10 says, "Two are better than one, because they have a good reward for their toil. For if they fall, one will lift up his fellow. But woe to him who is alone when he falls and has not another to lift him up!"

Don't isolate in your pain. I know there are times when we all want alone time. When we all need space to release the guttural cries or pleadings with God. But don't stay stuck there. Don't allow the Enemy to keep you in a place of seclusion. He knows you will heal and grow if you step out in faith and get around other believers, so his aim is to make you stay in that place of darkness. Fight against it. Allow yourself time to grieve, then wash your face, wipe your tears, get up off the floor, and show up.

Unanswered Questions

Why does God give us visions and dreams if we can't stop what's coming? It's a question I've grappled with so often, especially since losing River. When I talk to other parents who have lost children, I often ask them if they ever had a feeling, a thought, or a dream that their child's life might be cut short. It's surprising how many of them pause and then, with wide eyes, say, "Yes."

As parents, we all experience those everyday fears—the moments when our thoughts get the best of us and we imagine the worst—but what I'm talking about goes deeper. Some parents just know, somehow, that their child's time on earth will be brief. It's a feeling that defies earthly explanation. I always had a sense that River knew his time was short. I know that might sound strange, but he lived with an urgency and fearlessness that I couldn't quite explain. He talked about heaven constantly, telling his big sister that someday he would see a big T. rex in heaven, but he needed her to know that "it's nice, sissy, it's nice."

While Riv was still with us, I was reading *Hope Unfolding* by Becky Thompson one day, and she told a story about her little boy, who saw a man in a shop while they were out. He pleaded with his mom to go and ask the man if he knew who Jesus was. They had been discussing how some people know Jesus and some people don't, so it's important that they talk to people about Him and let them know that Jesus knows them and He loves them. The boy went over and was waving at the man, but then they left the café without asking the question the son so desperately wanted to ask.

They drove all the way home, still talking about the man, and Becky felt so convicted that they had to drive back to the café and make sure that he knew who Jesus was. On the way back she was prepping her son with what they would say if the man said he did know Jesus and what they would say if he didn't. If he said that he knew Jesus, they would say, "Jesus is my friend too!" and they would give him a high five. If the man said he didn't know Jesus, they would say, "He loves you very much!"

Upon returning to the café, she approached the man, saying something along the lines of "I'm sorry, we were just in here and my son was waving at you. He was very concerned that you may not know

Jesus, so we had to come all the way back up here to ask you." The man looked at her, over at her son, and said, "Buddy, come here. Give me a high five. Jesus is my friend." She was stunned that the man said and did exactly what *they* had planned to say and do![6]

We were still new to attending church back then. I hadn't put River in Sunday school or anything, and apart from singing "Jesus Loves Me" to Riv at night, we really hadn't had conversations about who Jesus was. I closed the book after reading that little story and, feeling convicted, went over to River as he was playing with toys on a mattress on the floor in our bedroom, and asked, "Hey, buddy, do you know who Jesus is?"

"Yes," he said confidently.

Surprised, I said, "You do?"

"Mm-hmm."

"Who is He, who is Jesus?"

Without missing a beat, he looked at me, smiled, and said, "Jesus is my friend." Literally the exact same thing that the man and the woman and child said in the story.

He was two.

The days before River passed, I noticed something different. Each night, as I rocked him, he wanted to hold on to me a little tighter. When I laid him down in his crib and turned to leave the room, he'd call out to me and with the biggest smile would say, "One more kiss, Mama!"—and it wasn't just one more. It was twenty "one more kisses" each night that week. I'm so thankful for those extra kisses now. They say one day you will do something for the last time and you won't know it's the last. I didn't know those were the last kisses I would get, but I am so thankful that God gifted me a few more than usual.

Granger and River would often visit the Yee Yee Farm, our family warehouse where we ship our outdoor apparel from. Just past the entrance up the gravel drive is a large pond with a big cement dock leading out to the water. This being Texas, you never knew if the pond would run dry, but that year it had been full. That dock always made me anxious because River couldn't swim yet. He and Granger would often walk out to feed the fish, their legs dangling over the edge. It terrified me. On one afternoon before River passed, we took him to the farm. It was a typical day there, and River would run around to each person and say hello. He would run to Uncle Ty Ty, then to Uncle Park Park. There were so many adults around, and each of us thought someone else was watching him. A few moments went by, and I had that sinking feeling—*Where's River?* We started searching the offices, but immediately my mind went to the pond. I ran to the car, jumped in, and sped down to the water, praying the entire time: *Please, God, please let him be safe. Please don't let him be in the water. Please, God.*

When I got there, the murky pond revealed nothing. My heart was pounding, and panic surged through me. What if he was in there and I couldn't see him? It seemed like a crazy thought that he could have gotten out the door and down to the pond that quickly, but my mind went there. I raced back to the warehouse, and as I pulled up, there was Granger, standing outside, holding River in his arms. I collapsed in my car, relieved and sobbing hysterically with my head buried in my hands on the steering wheel, struggling to catch my breath. I kept repeating, "Thank you, God. Thank you, God." River had been in another office with the door closed, playing with a little airplane on the floor. But that day stayed with me. Something about it felt like a foreshadowing I didn't fully understand.

And then on the day River died, we were driving that same road. I was sitting in the passenger seat, biting the skin around my nails— something I tend to do when I am deep in thought. Granger noticed and asked, "What are you thinking about?" Without hesitation, I said, "River drowning." He tried to reassure me: "Babe, don't you think if he fell in, I would see him and grab him?" But I couldn't shake the unease.

That evening I was relieved to be away from the farm and its pond. I had even scheduled swim lessons for the boys the following week—something that had been on my mind for a while. But then the very night I had mentioned River drowning, he did. Just a few hours later. Not in the farm pond I had always worried about. He drowned in our own pool. In our backyard. Inside the locked gate. One week before his scheduled swim lessons.

I couldn't understand it. Why had God given me that thought? Why was it the thought of the pond and not the pool? I struggled with this for so long, the why of it all. I shared my questions with a friend, and she offered me a perspective I hadn't considered. "Maybe God gave you that thought," she said, "so that when it happened, you'd have peace knowing it was Him." Again, I know that may sound bizarre to some, but I have held on to that.

If you're reading this and you've had similar experiences—moments when an unexplainable thought or feeling settled on you, perhaps even in a way that later felt like a foreshadowing of some kind—know that you're not alone. I've spoken to countless people who contended with this very thing. I spent countless hours wrestling with that thought I had about River. Why had it been so vivid? Was there something I missed? Or was God showing me something I couldn't have changed, no matter what I did? I didn't know. All I knew was that God is all-powerful and nothing happens outside of His control. If it wasn't River's time to depart, He would still be here. How do I know this? Because the Bible says God knows all of our days before we even live them. Psalm 139 is very clear:

> For you formed my inward parts;
>> you knitted me together in my mother's womb.
> I praise you, for I am fearfully and wonderfully made.
> Wonderful are your works;
>> my soul knows it very well.

My frame was not hidden from you,

when I was being made in secret,

> intricately woven in the depths of the earth.

Your eyes saw my unformed substance;

in your book were written, every one of them,

> the days that were formed for me,

> when as yet there was none of them. (vv. 13–16)

In His sovereignty (there's that word again), God sometimes does warn us directly, guiding us away from danger, and we can see this throughout Scripture. Joseph was warned in a dream to take Mary and baby Jesus to Egypt. Paul was cautioned not to go to certain cities because of imminent threats. These moments remind us that God actively watches over His children and does sometimes intervene to guide us toward safety or a different path.

But there are other times when He places something in our hearts—through a thought, dream, or feeling—and we may not fully understand its purpose. It might be that He's allowing us to sense something ahead, not so we can change the outcome but so we can later find peace in knowing He was always there, good or bad. The Bible gives examples of people receiving dreams or revelations about events they couldn't stop. Joseph's dreams in Genesis 37 about his future authority came true years later, but they also involved betrayal from his family, suffering, and separation—events he couldn't prevent. These dreams weren't given to Joseph so he could change his future but so that he would recognize God's hand through all the trials he would face. After all that he went through—being sold into slavery, wrongly accused, and thrown into prison—he came out in a place of acknowledgment that the Lord had sent him ahead for the saving of many lives (Genesis 45:7–8). The Bible repeatedly emphasizes that God is sovereign over all events, knowing the beginning from the end. Isaiah 45 speaks so much to this:

I am the LORD, and there is no other.

I form light and create darkness;

    I make well-being and create calamity;

    I am the LORD, who does all these things. (vv. 6–7)

That sovereignty means that He is fully aware of every detail of our lives, so if you have felt these moments, you are not alone. God, in His eternal wisdom, knows every step we will take, and while He sometimes directs us away from danger, other times He walks with us right through it, holding our hearts even as He allows us to walk through pain and suffering.

Even when we don't understand why or how these moments fit into God's bigger plan, we can lean on the promise that every single one of our days is in His hands, and as we read in Romans 8:28, "We know that for those who love God all things work together for good, for those who are called according to his purpose." This reassures us that even things we cannot change or prevent are woven into His loving plan.

It doesn't answer all the questions, but it does give me a sense of peace. I don't fully understand why God gives us thoughts or dreams when we really don't have as much control as it would seem or when we can't change what's coming. But perhaps, in His mercy, He prepares our hearts so that when the unthinkable happens, we know He's still there. That even in our deepest pain and our hardest questions, we are not alone and nothing takes Him by surprise.

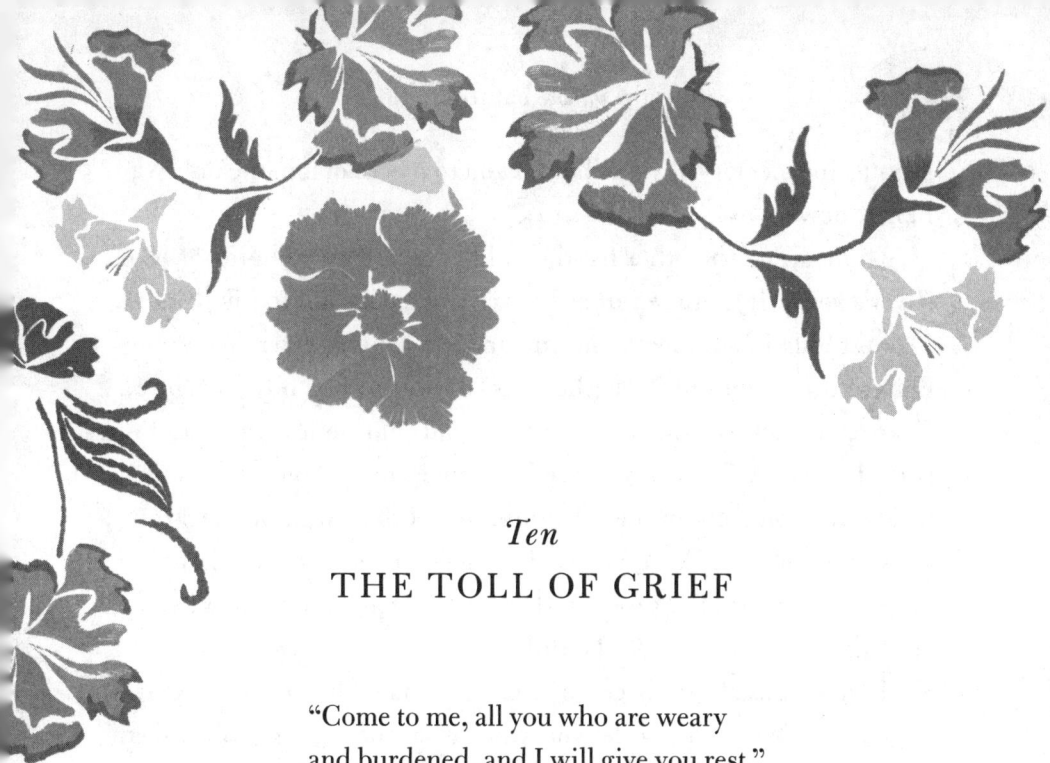

Ten

THE TOLL OF GRIEF

"Come to me, all you who are weary
and burdened, and I will give you rest."
Matthew 11:28 NIV

Grief takes its toll in ways that are as unique as the people experiencing it. After River died, each of us in the family handled our grief very differently. For me, the bathroom became my refuge. I would retreat, shut the door, and let the tears come, muffling my cry into towels or pressing my face into the cold tile. Sometimes, I'd sit on the carpet of the closet, my head in my knees, praying. The shower, the bathtub, the car—these became places where I could release the overwhelming sadness in secret. Come to think of it, I probably cried over every square inch of central Texas pouring out my lament. Night after night, I watched videos of River, clinging to anything I had left of his precious voice and sweet face. It was my way of feeling close to him, of keeping his memory alive, of holding on to pieces of him the only way I knew how.

Granger, on the other hand, couldn't bear to see photos or hear River's voice. It shattered him. I never wanted to add to his pain, so I would hide in another room, turning the volume down low on my phone so he wouldn't hear the sweet sound of our boy's laughter. Granger's grief was quieter, more internal, but no less intense, I'm sure. I worried for him because he seemed to be holding so much inside. It's common for men, I think, to feel they must be the strong ones, the rocks that keep everything together. But I feared that if he didn't allow himself to process what he was feeling, it might all come crashing down one day. And it did.

London has always been our emotional one. She's passionate like her daddy but will always let you know what she's feeling. She asked so many questions, her tears often flowing as she talked about how much she missed her little brother. Nights were the hardest for her; she would cry before bed, struggling to make sense of it all, saying she couldn't get River's purple cheeks out of her mind. She told me one night that she thought God saved River from something more serious in his future.

"Maybe something bad was coming for River, Mama. I think God saved him from something worse in his life." I welcomed that thought.

Little children at school would make comments to her that hurt. They told her they saw River drown on TV (really, they saw a reenactment that the news stations created), or they would tell her if she didn't play what they wanted to play, they would talk about River to try to make her sad. We tried to pray through it all and give them grace. I reminded her that they were just kids, too, and sometimes kids don't think before they speak. I would often get a call from the nurse that London had a tummy ache, something we later found out was more anxiety than sickness. She also developed motor tics around this time, involuntary movements throughout her body. They started in her hands, then moved to her eyebrows, eyes, neck, and back. We still aren't sure if the trauma of losing River is what caused them. They have subsided a lot, but every now and then when she gets angry or excited or has too much sugar, they ramp back up again.

Lincoln, our little comedian, still so small, held a lot of his emotion in. To this day, I can remember only a handful of times when he's really broken down. One of those times was when we were driving by the cemetery where River is laid to rest. It was a year after his passing, and as we drove by, we said, "Bye, River, we love you," and suddenly, Lincoln lost it. He wailed uncontrollably. He cried so hard I had to pull over and hold him for about fifteen minutes, just letting him release all the pain he had kept inside. We all sat there and cried, hazards on, stopped on the old country back road a few miles from River's grave. Lincoln didn't talk much about his little brother, but I would find pictures he drew of him and River playing together or of River with wings in a photo he drew of the sky, or occasionally I would find blocks laid out in his room that spelled out his little brother's name. He would ask questions at night about death. He was often scared he would die in his sleep and wondered if it would hurt.

When Granger's book *Like a River* came out, he was looking at the section of photos in the center of the book and came to one photo of all of River's tractors and toys lying around the old tire we had in the backyard. The area where we were when we told the kids that River died. We left it the way River left it, and I took a photo so we would have a memory of that space. River played there all the time, scooping up dirt with his toy dump trucks and excavators. Lincoln got really quiet as his eyes came to that page. Something about that picture struck him and he began to sob. "That's so sad," he said as he closed the book. We held him for a long time and he let out some pent-up sadness that needed to be released.

People often ask me for advice on how to walk through pain with loved ones and children, and the best thing I can say is this: Have grace. Have grace for how they're feeling, even if it's different from how you're processing your own grief. One day, one of you might feel like you're finally finding some light, while the other is still deep in the darkness. One of you might need to look at photos and talk about your loved one, while the other can't bear it. One child might act as if nothing has changed, while the other weeps constantly.

All of these reactions are natural, normal, and okay. Grief is an intensely individual experience, and it's important to allow each person to process their pain in their own way, as long as it's not harmful to themselves or others. I can only share what worked for us, but we still very much kept River a part of our lives. We kept photos up in the house, we talked about him regularly, we let the kids play with River's toys. We didn't make his room a shrine or say his belongings were off-limits.

I've heard from others who have lost siblings say to us what a blessing it was that we were keeping River's memory alive and were letting our children say his name and play with his things. Some people we talked to were never able to properly grieve someone they lost because their parents took down every photo, shut the door to their room, never let anyone inside, and told the siblings not even to say the name because it hurt too much. Only years later when they were adults were they able to properly grieve that loss, but they still carried resentment toward their parents from years before.

Intimacy

I hesitate to open up about my intimacy with Granger in this space, but this is all shared with his permission. I feel it's important for married couples to talk about or be prepared for how a marriage is impacted when navigating the deep waters of grief. The statistics for parents staying together after losing a child are not in our favor. It takes work—real, intentional work, sacrifice, and selflessness—to keep a marriage strong through something so devastating. It takes both of you choosing each other, even when everything inside you may want to bail.

Intimacy, in all its forms, is a part of a healthy marriage. The Lord beautifully designed us for this—marriage as a covenant, a union, and picture that reflects His love for the church. He created intimacy as a way for us to draw closer to each other, offering comfort, vulnerability, and strength even in the hardest seasons. And while it doesn't always mean sex, that connection is still a significant piece of the puzzle.

When you're facing unimaginable pain, heartache, or the stress that comes with loss, a diagnosis, financial worries, or caring for a child with special needs, intimacy with your spouse is often the furthest thing from your mind. But early on, I realized something crucial: The Enemy would use any means to attack my marriage, and I didn't want to lose Granger and what we had on top of losing River. I love Granger with every part of me. We had a wonderful marriage before all of this—a deep, loving connection, both emotionally and physically. He truly is my best friend.

I don't remember exactly how long it was after River passed, but one night we were lying in bed, and Granger kissed me. It was tender, slow, almost hesitant, as if he was asking for permission to bridge the distance that had grown between us. He wasn't forcing anything; he was giving me the space to decide if I was ready. I looked at him, assuring him that this was okay, and I told him, "I love you, first and foremost. You're still my husband."

It felt strange, almost wrong, to allow myself to feel any sort of pleasure or joy in that moment. But as we made love for the first time since that awful night, it was sweet and tender, and honestly, we both needed it. We needed to remember that despite the tragedy, we were still us. Afterward, I quietly cried myself to sleep. It was a confusing mix of endorphins and sadness, swirling together. But it was a step in connecting I knew we both needed and wanted. I knew he was grieving not only for himself but for losing a part of his wife, for the woman I was before this happened.

You may be hurting right now, and the thought of being close to your spouse might feel impossible. Grief has a way of making us want to isolate and put up walls, even from the person who is experiencing the same loss, but you will need each other more than ever if you are walking through something tragic. If I can offer any encouragement, it's this: Fight for that intimacy. Fight for those small touches, the simple hugs, the quick back rubs, kisses, and hand holds. It doesn't have to only be about bedroom intimacy, but don't let grief drive a wedge between you. In those moments of connection, even the smallest ones, you're reminded that you're not alone in this—that you're in it together, still holding on to each other through the storm.

I know in this day and age it doesn't seem like many people value the sanctity of marriage anymore, but you made a commitment before God and to each other. "For better or worse" isn't just a phrase you said at your wedding—it's one of the foundations of your life together, a vow that you would stick it out through thick and thin. And right now you may be facing a "worse" part in your story. But part of the beauty of life together is that weathering the storms hand in hand can lead to a deeper connection if you both fight for it. You can come out of a devastating season even stronger, not in spite of the pain, but because of it.

Your marriage can survive child loss, financial struggles, wayward children, even adultery if you both commit to staying connected and pursuing Christ together. It requires intentionality, repentance, forgiveness, and grace. It's not easy, and it won't happen overnight, but if you choose to lean into each other instead of away—to really love and sacrifice for each other, even in the throes of unimaginable pain— you'll find that your marriage can not only survive but thrive. You'll develop a deeper bond, one that's been forged in the fire of hardship and one that speaks as a gospel witness to others around you. So, fight for each other. Even on the days when it feels impossible, choose to hold on, and trust that God can rebuild what's been broken.

Therapy

The air in Cumberland Furnace, Tennessee, felt thick and crisp in mid-November. Five months after we buried River, Granger and I arrived at Onsite, an intensive therapy retreat in the middle of a lush forest, surrounded by towering trees and the stillness of nature. The retreat felt like a haven, with rustic cabins, a crackling old fireplace, and large wooden bookshelves full of well-worn books. We had come here as a gift

Trust that God can rebuild what's been broken.

from friends (who kindly covered the cost for us), not entirely sure what to expect and not sure if it would even help, but we were grateful for the gift and we wanted to do all we could to grow and heal.

When we first arrived, they took our phones. We were cut off from the outside world, forced to face the rawness of our emotions without distraction. It was actually nice, aside from having no contact with the kids for a week, but we both knew they needed strong parents—parents who were fighting for each other, for joy, and for healing. One wall of our room had a sign that struck me: "What happens to a man is less significant than what happens within him." Something had happened to us and something was definitely happening within us. As I was reading devotionals and walking through this pain, I kept being led to Isaiah 43:19: "Behold, I am doing a new thing; now it springs forth, do you not perceive it? I will make a way in the wilderness and rivers in the desert." Something new was happening in our lives, and we were beginning to see we were powerless to stop it.

When we met for group therapy, we were told not to share names or talk about who we were or what we did outside that space. Celebrities, musicians, businesspeople, moms and dads were all stripped of titles and worldly status, defined instead by our stories of pain. There were so many layers of sorrow—child loss, sexual abuse, toxic relationships, even murder. It was like we were all soldiers returning from battle, broken but searching for hope in the valley of death. We ate together, played games, and, slowly, began to open our hearts to one another. By the end of the week, we knew each other's names, our stories, our brokenness. We cried together, prayed for one another, and began to form a bond that felt like family.

Our therapy sessions were both emotional and illuminating. We did exercises where we chose art and photos that mirrored the state of our hearts, both then and where we wanted them to be. In one exercise where Granger and I had to work together, one of us was blindfolded and had to talk, while the other had no blindfold but couldn't speak. The goal was to get from one place to another, guiding each other with nothing but our actions and words. We laughed and worked well together, surprising the counselors with our teamwork after what we had been through. We showed up to Onsite for healing from the loss of our son, but we ended up learning things about our marriage in the process. I learned I needed to use my voice more, and Granger needed to let me carry some of the weight.

That realization came during an outdoor exercise on a rope cable. The goal was to get from one side to the other without breaking contact or falling. The cables started close together, easy enough to manage. But as they widened, we had to lean into each other for support; not letting go meant both of us needed to lean more parallel to the ground. At one point, Granger was carrying too much, and I was too silent, not telling him what I needed. We were about to fall when the counselor urged me to speak up. "Amber, tell him what you need!" So I yelled, "Give me some of your weight!" As soon as he did, we found balance and made it across without letting go of each other.

We then split up for our individual sessions, and it was my day for a technique called brain spotting, a form of therapy designed to access and process trauma stored deep in the brain. Sometimes known as EMDR, brain spotting involves focusing on a specific point or memory while the therapist helps guide you through the emotions and sensations tied to that experience in an attempt to close the loop that often occurs in people suffering from PTSD and trauma.

I sat across from the therapist, eyes fixed on a small pointer he had in the air. He would move it from side to side as I spoke, retelling the story of June 4. He asked me to take note of changes in my breathing or heartbeat as my eyes followed the pointer. As I focused and recalled the worst night of my life, the images began to flood in, the haunting slideshow that played in endless loops—the night River died; his lifeless, purple body; Granger's terror-stricken face as he tried CPR; the panic; the chaos. I could feel it all again, like it was happening right then.

Marc, my counselor, gently guided me through it, his voice calm as tears filled his eyes and mine. I was deep in the memory now, recalling every excruciating detail of River's death. And then, suddenly, the room went dark. The lights shut off completely.

We both froze, our eyes locking in the dimness.

"That's never happened before," he said softly, his voice barely audible.

A few seconds passed, and just as suddenly, the lights flickered back on. I couldn't help but smile through my tears, because it felt like a Godwink. (I'll explain that more in a bit.) In that moment, all I could think of was River. He used to love flipping the lights on and off at home, giggling as he did it, lighting up the room with his joy. I thought about the lightning storm we had witnessed shortly after his burial—how the sky had lit up in brilliant flashes for what seemed like an hour. It wasn't just any storm. It was lightning like I'd never seen before, bolts shooting sideways across the sky, illuminating the darkness with electric colored light. The kids were outside, watching in awe, shouting, "Do it again, River!"

Flash! It would happen again and again, lighting up the whole sky. We didn't want to go inside until the beautiful show was over.

I know it wasn't River flipping the lights in that therapy room, but in my heart, it felt like a small, tender moment of comfort—another wink from heaven in the midst of the pain.

The retreat wasn't a magical fix. There is no quick, magical fix for hurt. We didn't walk out of there healed. But it gave us tools—tools to navigate the sorrow that we came to understand was just part of living in this broken world. And it made me realize how many others around us are hurting, grieving, carrying their own burdens, even when we don't see it. There are people in our workplaces, our schools, in line right next to us at the grocery store or the stoplight, all struggling in ways we may never know.

The Battle for Joy

As we left Tennessee and returned to our lives, I knew that while loss would always be part of our story, it didn't have to be our identity or define our future. There was hope, and it was waiting to break through, like those flashes of lightning in the dark. I felt lighter when I returned home from that trip, and in my journal from that time I wrote,

> *I am feeling such a sense of calm and I am breathing deeper than I have in months.*

The trip didn't stop my tears, though. I still cried every single day. Counseling, therapy, and medication are all wonderful tools to have, especially for anyone struggling with pain, addiction, abuse, betrayal, grief, or depression. I am so thankful for the expertise of the staff at our retreat, and I deeply appreciate doctors, modern medicines, and treatments that aim to guide us and get us back on track. But they offer only a temporary peace. A temporary calm. A Band-Aid on a bullet hole in a lot of cases. These can be wonderful additions in our healing when needed, but the true healing, the kind that reaches the deepest parts of our broken hearts, doesn't come from anything this world can provide. It comes from the true peace, the lasting peace, that only Jesus offers. "Peace I leave with you; my peace I give to you. Not as the world gives do I give to you. Let not your hearts be troubled, neither let them be afraid" (John 14:27).

Even though we were doing the hard, messy work of moving forward, we still ached for our child. My journal entries would detail how often I would cry alone in the bathroom:

> *I struggled a lot this week. I miss River so much; I miss his funny wit and sweet hugs. I still don't understand and my heart is broken. I'm trying to be strong for London and Lincoln but I find myself hiding in closets and the bathroom crying so hard. Lord help me. Help me to walk by faith. Help me to know this is all for your glory. I know you are with me, I feel it, I see it, I hear it. Help me remember this. It's hard. I'm so sad and I can't do this alone. I need you. In Jesus' name, amen.*

In the GriefShare group I mentioned in an earlier chapter, we would often talk about ambushes—those moments when grief sneaks up and hits you out of nowhere. You think you're doing okay, holding it together, and then *bam*—something small, something seemingly insignificant, knocks you off your feet, bringing you back to day one.

One day, I opened the fridge and saw a cup of FAGE yogurt. It was River's favorite; he called it "Ma's yodurt" (Mama's yogurt). It was cherry, and we always shared it while curled up watching *PJ Masks* or *PAW Patrol*. I stood there, staring at that yogurt cup, and cried. I wouldn't ever be sharing my yogurt with him again. I cried over yogurt.

Another time, I went to grab donuts for the big kids. River used to come with me every Saturday, kicking his legs in excitement for his "baby donuts," the little glazed donut holes he loved so much. When I pulled up to the window, the owner smiled at me and peeked into the back seat, looking for him. My stomach sank. *Why did I come here? Of course, she would ask. She saw him every weekend. Please don't ask, please don't ask.*

"Where's your baby?" she asked, her eyes searching the back of the car.

I felt the lump in my throat rise. *Here we go.* I wanted to tell her he's in heaven, but the words were barely a whisper. "He's in heaven," I said softly. *Why didn't you just say he was at home?!*

She didn't hear me. Leaning in closer, she smiled. "Where is he?"

I swallowed hard and said it again. "He died. He's in heaven."

Her face fell. "Oh . . . my, what happened?"

I wanted to disappear. "He drowned," I said, feeling the shame wash over me. There is often unspoken judgment that comes with the word *drowning*. Everyone thinks you're a neglectful parent when your child drowns. I felt like I had to justify myself, to defend my love for him, to explain how it happened, but it wasn't the time or place, and I just didn't have it in me to talk anymore.

Her voice softened. "I'm so sorry," she said as she handed me my order.

I nodded a thank-you, tears burning my eyes as I pulled away from the drive-thru. I haven't been back to that Shipley since.

The ambushes of grief can knock us off course a bit, but the opposite of that—the Godwinks I mentioned before, those sweet moments of unexpected comfort—can remind us that we're seen and loved, often carrying us through and giving us just a little boost of strength in any given moment.

I experienced a lot of Godwinks after we lost River. On his birthday or his angel day we would often see incredible rainbows stretched across the sky, reminding us of God's presence, promise, and comfort. Another time, as I was taking a shower, crying as the water ran down my back, I looked up to see a tiny cloud shaped like a perfect heart right out of the window. It was there right when I needed it and then disappeared in seconds.

Another powerful Godwink happened when I was driving near our old house. I came to a stoplight, and catty-corner to me was the community swimming pool, filled with children laughing and playing. I instantly felt sad as I thought about what River must have felt in the water. Was he scared? Did he try to cry for me? Was he in pain? But just then, a car pulled in front of me, blocking my entire view of the pool. Written in shoe polish in large white letters on the back driver-side window were the words "Jesus Loves You." I mean, what are the odds of that?! Right in that moment? Immediately, my focus shifted. I whispered, "Thank you, Lord," and the light turned green.

But my biggest Godwink came in October 2019. I was a mess one night, praying and pleading with God. My heart was so heavy, and I begged Him to give me a sign—a tangible reminder that River was safe with Him and that he wasn't in pain when he died. I don't know why, but a blue butterfly came to my mind. Through my tears, I prayed, *Please, God, please show me a blue butterfly so I know. Please. I am so sorry I am asking, but I need something. Please, God. Please help me.* I cried myself to sleep again that night.

The next morning was just another regular day as a mom. But as I stepped outside, I was startled to see something eerie: seventeen buzzards perched on our roof. Seventeen. I stood there, watching them for a long time, and even called Granger to come see. I chuckled to myself, thinking, *God's got jokes.* "Well, it's not a blue butterfly, but it's something," I mumbled as I walked off.

"What?" Granger asked.

"Oh, nothing. I was really sad last night and asked God for a sign. I asked Him for a blue butterfly. I know it was silly."

Later that day, I went to the UPS Store to pick up some mail. As I reached into our mailbox and pulled out the letters, I froze. Right on top was an envelope with a big, beautiful blue butterfly stamp. Across the front, the words "Thinking of you" were written.

Some might call it coincidence or luck, but as I have come to study the Scriptures, I've learned there are no coincidences with God, only divine appointments. The Bible tells us that He is a part of every detail of our lives.

That letter had already been on the way before I even prayed. God had already set things in motion. As the Scriptures remind us, "O LORD, you have searched me and known me! You know when I sit down and when I rise up; you discern my thoughts from afar. You search out my path and my lying down and are acquainted with all my ways. Even before a word is on my tongue, behold, O LORD, you know it altogether" (Psalm 139:1–4), and "Before they call I will answer; while they are yet speaking I will hear" (Isaiah 65:24). Matthew 10:29–31 states, "Are not two sparrows sold for a penny? And not one of them will fall to the ground apart from your Father. But even the hairs on your head are all numbered. Fear not, therefore; you are of more value than many sparrows." God cares about you! He is in the details of your life.

I feel like I should be careful here in talking about these things because in our fallen nature, we can come to depend on them. We can seek the things God created and believe that our dead loved ones sent them to us. We can falsely think that our deceased grandmother is showing up as a cardinal by our window. Or that people that have passed on are sending us signs from the grave. It is unbiblical and spiritually dangerous to believe that we are receiving signs directly from loved ones who are no longer with us, such as thinking they are communicating with us from heaven, because this belief can open the door to deception and demonic influence. The Bible is clear that when people die, they do not return to communicate with the living (Job 7:9–10). Attempting to interpret signs or engage with spiritual realms can invite demonic forces, which often masquerade as comforting or familiar spirits. Scripture warns us about such practices, such as in Deuteronomy 18:10–12, which forbids seeking communication with the dead, as it is considered detestable to the Lord.

The Enemy can exploit our grief and vulnerability by presenting counterfeit experiences or signs that seem to come from our loved ones but are meant to draw us away from the truth of God's Word. Engaging in practices like seeking after signs from the dead can blur our discernment and lead us into a form of idolatry, where we place more emphasis on signs and experiences than on God Himself.

However, in His care and love, God can bring comfort to us through His creation. He may use nature—such as a beautiful sunrise, a bird, a rainbow, or a quiet moment of peace—as a gentle reminder of His presence and comfort during our grief. This kind of comfort must point us back to Him, the Creator and the ultimate source of peace and healing, rather than leading us to misplace our trust in mystical signs.

The key difference is that true comfort from the Lord will draw us nearer to Him and will align with His Word, while false signs or spiritual experiences can turn our focus away from God. It's important to guard our hearts and rely on the Word of God as the ultimate authority for truth and comfort. True peace and

God can bring comfort to us through His creation.

reassurance come from knowing that our loved ones who have trusted in Christ are in the Lord's care and that He is the only one who brings lasting comfort and hope.

Jesus reassured us of this in John 14:1–3, saying,

> "Let not your hearts be troubled. Believe in God; believe also in me. In my Father's house are many rooms. If it were not so, would

I have told you that I go to prepare a place for you? And if I go and prepare a place for you, I will come again and will take you to myself, that where I am you may be also."

So, dear sister or brother, let not your heart be troubled. If you have trusted in Christ, He has gone before you to prepare a place for you. He is your comfort and hope in a world full of sorrow, sin, and death. In Him, we find the assurance that He is with us now and will one day bring us into eternal joy in His presence.

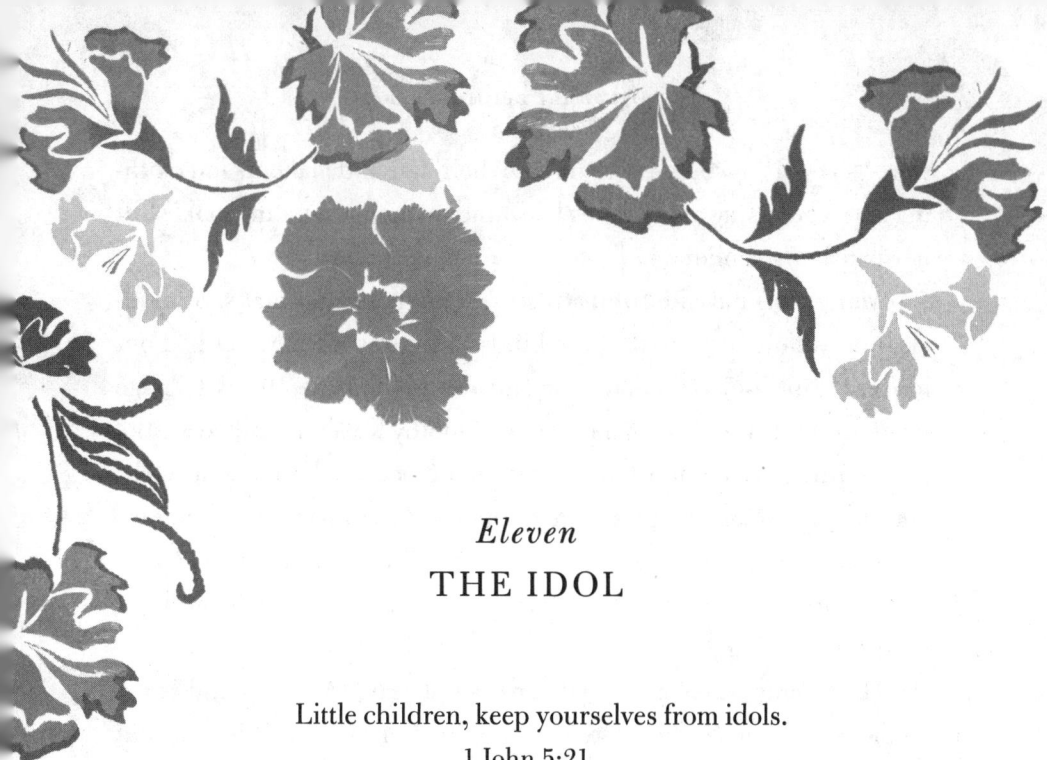

Eleven

THE IDOL

Little children, keep yourselves from idols.
1 John 5:21

When you think of the word idol, *what comes to mind? Maybe it's a* celebrity you looked up to as a child. Maybe it's an incredible athlete you admire or maybe, if you grew up in the '80s, the only thing that comes to mind is the name Billy. I grew up in the Britney Spears era. I can't tell you how many times I played her debut CD, windows down in my electric-blue Plymouth Laser, blond hair blowing in the wind, probably driving way too fast around my neighborhood as a teenager. Pop music was big in our house. My mom and I would record ourselves singing Madonna songs in my room on an old cassette player. I even had a life-size poster of Donnie Wahlberg from New Kids on the Block hanging on the back of my door. I wouldn't have used the term *idol* back then, but I definitely thought the artists on MTV and VH1 were "so cool." I would try to imitate their hair and makeup and clothing and would sing and dance all around my house with my makeshift hairbrush microphone.

Many of us have idolized athletes, celebrities, musicians, or models, and we often think of these kinds of figures when we talk about idolatry. But idolatry is far more insidious than the 1990s teenage posters on the wall. Pastor and author Timothy Keller described an idol as "anything more important to you than God, anything that absorbs your heart and imagination more than God, anything you seek to give you what only God can give. A counterfeit god is anything so central and essential to your life that, should you lose it, your life would feel hardly worth living."[1]

How many times have we heard people say, "My husband is my whole world" or "My children are my life" or "I would die without them"? How many of us have placed the things of creation above the Creator? Many things in our life that we love are very good things, but it's when they become *ultimate* things that we begin to get into danger.

Throughout Scripture, God warns us about idolatry. Idols don't just affect our spiritual health; they slowly rob us of our joy in Him. In Exodus 20:4–5, we read the command, "You shall not make for yourself a carved image, or any likeness of anything that is in heaven above, or that is in the earth beneath, or that is in the water under the earth."

This past summer we studied the book of Judges in our churchwide Bible study. I was able to give a talk to the women in our congregation on unseen idols in our lives. We discussed the story of Samson, the sixth major judge raised up to begin to deliver the people of Israel. Samson was set apart from birth. He was made a Nazirite by the Lord, and he was to follow the Nazirite vows, but we quickly see that Samson began to abandon all those vows by trusting in his own strength and power. Though he didn't worship the Baals or pagan gods, he did struggle with unseen idols of the heart. Samson was a man who loved women and sex and power and comfort. And his idols ended up leading him to bondage and blindness, both figuratively and literally.

Idolatry is not just about bowing down to carved images or golden calves like in Exodus 32. Today's idols are more subtle, more internal, just like Samson's. In Ezekiel 14:3, God says, "These men have taken their idols into their hearts, and set the stumbling block of their iniquity before their faces."

French theologian John Calvin stated that the human heart is "a perpetual forge of idols."[2] Our sinful hearts are still perpetual idol factories. It might not look like melted-down jewelry and golden calves, but it's just as dangerous, maybe even more so because we don't always recognize it. Our modern idols sneak in through things like wealth, comfort, materialism, sports, technology, relationships—even body image.

Think about it: How much time do we spend staring at these little six-inch devices in our hands? These phones easily become idols, eating up hours in the day that could be spent in God's Word. We find ourselves constantly seeking validation through likes, comments, and followers, and we start to base our self-worth on how we are perceived by others online. We scroll endlessly, filling our minds with things that distract us from the One who truly deserves our devotion.

Or take youth sports or college football. When sports begin to dominate our schedules, they can push aside time for worship, prayer, and gathering with the church community. Many families find themselves on the road every weekend, missing Sunday services and fellowship with the body. If the demands of the sport start to outweigh the time spent nurturing our relationship with God, it can signal that the sport is becoming an idol.

Corrie ten Boom and other speakers and pastors have said, "If the devil can't make you bad, he'll make you busy." The Enemy's tactics aren't always about pulling us into obvious sin. Instead, he uses distraction, busyness, and the many demands of life to draw our focus away from God.

Our modern culture may not bow to carved statues, but we are still guilty of bowing our hearts to things we treasure more than Jesus. I have to check my own heart daily on this. The good things in our lives—our children, our health, our work, our activities—can easily become idols when they take the place of our devotion to God.

Sometimes, the idols we create are false versions of God Himself. How often have we heard this idea of a God who just wants us to be happy, healthy, and wealthy? That's not the God of Scripture. The God of the Bible calls us to holiness and repentance, not to a life of pleasure, comfort, and ease.

Idols don't just distract us—they enslave us. We become bound to what we worship. Instead of living freely as children of the King, we're left exhausted, constantly striving for more, always searching to fill the void. And the more we pursue these things, the further we drift from the only One who can satisfy the deepest longings of our hearts. As our devotion to idols grows, our relationship with God suffers. We stop seeking Him first. We stop spending time in His presence. Slowly but surely, we forget who we are in Him. We become so busy chasing after empty promises and comforts that we lose touch with the truth: In Christ, we have everything we need—peace, joy, purpose, and fulfillment. I hadn't seen that yet.

Idols don't just distract us—they enslave us.

One of the most shattering realizations in my grief was about to unfold, and once again, it happened on my bathroom floor. As I sat there crying, utterly consumed by sorrow, the Lord interrupted my pain with three words that changed everything. They weren't audible, but I felt every word, crushing my spirit, like a careful heart surgeon cutting through the fog of my despair with piercing clarity: *Enough. Seek Me.* These weren't my own thoughts, and as crazy as it may sound, they carried a weight I can't fully explain.

In that moment, God revealed an uncomfortable truth: I had made

River an idol in my life. My pain, my longing for him, my constant thoughts of him—they had begun to eclipse the One who is the source of all comfort and peace. Gently but firmly, the Lord was calling me to lift my eyes from my sadness and refocus them on Him.

Enough. Seek Me. It was a conviction, a call, and a challenge all at once. God was calling me to get up, to arise off the bathroom floor—both physically and spiritually. I felt in that moment that everyone is suffering something. I felt the Spirit saying to me, *Enough. Seek Me. Give Me the glory that belongs to Me alone.*

That moment marked the beginning of *Arise with Amber*. What started as a weekly YouTube show and has since become a podcast was born out of that pivotal encounter. It was the Lord calling me to arise, to share, and to point others to the only One who can bring healing in the midst of our brokenness. Those three words weren't just for me—they're for anyone lost in the depths of their pain. *Enough. Seek Me.* I pray they can be a call for you too.

It's a hard thing to realize that even our children, whom we love with every fiber of our beings, can become idols if we aren't careful. Or what if your career has become your identity? What happens when those precious things are actually taken from us? What happens when we're left grieving them? If we've made them the center of our universe, we've displaced our love and devotion to God, the only One who should be at the center. We must check our hearts daily and pray for the Lord to reveal any grievous way in us (Psalm 139:23-24).

My idol had become my son. I didn't realize it at first, but in my pain and grief, I had placed River at the center of my world, above everything else—including God. And it made me wonder: What about you? What have you unknowingly let become an idol in your life? Maybe it's your own kids, maybe it's your income or your image or politics. Maybe it's the other things I listed above. We all have something that at one time or another has gotten in the way of our devotion to the one true King. Pastor and theologian Jonathan Edwards wrote,

God is the highest good of the reasonable creature. The enjoyment of him is our proper; and is the only happiness with which our souls can be satisfied. To go to heaven, fully to enjoy God, is infinitely better than the most pleasant accommodations here. Better than fathers and mothers, husbands, wives, or children, or the company of any, or all earthly friends. These are but shadows; but the enjoyment of God is the substance. These are but scattered beams; but God is the sun. These are but streams; but God is the fountain. These are but drops, but God is the ocean.[3]

His Light in the Darkness

I've always been careful not to compare trauma. Each person's pain and grief are extremely personal and unique. Whether it's the loss of a spouse or a beloved pet, or a difficult divorce; walking through cancer with a loved one; or caring for a medically ill family member, any of these experiences can break someone's heart and turn their world upside down. But the loss of a child—it's been said by some to be the most severe form of grief. It feels out of sync with how life is supposed to work. We expect to bury our parents. We know that pets don't live forever. But burying your child? It feels unnatural and shatters everything we thought we knew, like it defies the order of life.

Granger and I knew from the moment we lost River that we didn't want our family to become another statistic. We stood together in that hospital garden and made a quiet, nonromantic agreement—we would choose each other, daily, no matter how hard it got. We wouldn't let anything tear our family apart. But the reality was that this was a storm we had never faced before. We honestly didn't know what life would look like moving forward. The closest pain we'd known was when Granger's dad, Chris, passed away suddenly in 2014.

That was an awful day. My mother-in-love, Debbee, had been at our house helping with our two little ones: London, two at the time, and newborn Lincoln. She stayed an extra day with us because that's just who she is—always giving, always there when you need her. The day she left, I grabbed a take-and-bake pizza (something Granger hasn't eaten in the ten years since we got the call), and we settled in on the couch as a family to watch *American Idol* (ironic, I know). Then the phone rang.

"Hello," Granger answered. I saw his face change as he walked into the little front living area of our home. I followed him in and he kept repeating, "Not yet. I'm not ready yet. It's too soon." Over and over.

"What's wrong?" I quietly mouthed. I thought maybe by his emotion something must have happened to his grandmother, Mini, or his sweet pup Rio.

"Dad . . . he had a heart attack."

"Is he okay?"

He shook his head. "No," he whispered. "He died."

It couldn't be. Not Chris.

Chris was the first real loss we experienced as a family, and it was a massive blow. Chris was such an incredible man. He was a man of integrity. He loved his wife. He loved his three boys. He loved the simple life, working on the ranch, drinking black coffee, and making friends with anyone he came in contact with. He gave the best hugs, and he had the best laugh. He and I loved a lot of the same things, like egg salad and mustang grapes, and we were the lucky ones who got the dark meat of the turkey all to ourselves at Thanksgiving because everyone else preferred the white. I couldn't wait for the kids to grow up with him as their grandpa. I looked forward to the days when he would teach them all about the different types of flowers and birds in Texas, fishing and hunting, how to plant a garden, and just life in general. If I ached from the loss of such a wonderful man, I could only imagine the pain my mother-in-love, husband, and my two brothers-in-love were walking through.

Chris was one of the first people to truly share Scripture with me. People had talked about Jesus in conversations before, but it was more topical; it wasn't the sharing of God's Word. One day in 2012, just a few months after London was born, we were sitting in his truck talking about hard things in life. Granger was on his hundred-mile walk. Each year he would walk one hundred miles in combat boots from Austin to Fort Hood to show his support for men and women in uniform. We were the pace car that would park ahead, stocked up with waters and snacks and Band-Aids for the walkers' blistered feet. I shared stories of what my brother was walking through in addiction and how I was struggling in my relationship with my own dad, and Chris shared stories of when he was younger and the verse he clung to in times of hardship. With moist eyes he spoke 2 Corinthians 12:9: "But he said to me, 'My grace is sufficient for you, for my power is made perfect in weakness.' Therefore, I will boast all the more gladly of my weaknesses, so that the power of Christ may rest upon me."

I wasn't walking with the Lord yet, but I admired and trusted Chris. I tucked that verse away in my heart, never knowing how much I would need it in the years to come.

As our family grieved the loss of Chris, I didn't quite know how to be there for Granger. I had never faced a loss of that magnitude or walked with someone through deep suffering. I was scared to talk about his dad for fear of upsetting him if he was having a "good" day. But I see now, after losing Riv, that I should have talked about Chris more in those early days of loss. Sometimes the silence is even more painful than potentially upsetting someone in a moment. I love talking about River and I love when anyone asks me about him. I've learned we don't always have to tiptoe around someone's pain. I still cry sometimes over losing Chris, and it's been a decade. I had a dream about him not long ago. I was sitting at the kitchen table and he walked up behind me and wrapped his big arms around my neck and said, "I'm so proud of you." I can't wait to see him again someday.

In the months after we lost Riv, I could tell Granger was hurting, but he was always so good at putting on a brave face and getting back to work. He got good at going through the motions of life, returning to the road just three weeks after the funeral. I didn't see his private moments in his truck or alone in the shower. I am sure he shed tears in all the places I did. But from the outside it looked like he was keeping it all bottled up.

Granger has always been passionate in whatever he does. It's something I love and admire about him. I always joke with him because when he gets on a kick about something, it's all he can think about. There's been World War II fascination and study, gardening, and beekeeping. At one point he was even obsessed with light bulbs. Currently it's propagating plants in our house, collecting and raising acorns, enjoying this new coffee he found, and taking ice baths.

But during this time, he was really into self-help books, getting in shape, meditating, journaling, visualizing, counting his macros, all the things he felt he could do on his own to make himself better. But none of it stopped the visions of that awful day, and the guilt still haunted him. The idol of self is easily one of the most deceptive idols we face. We can fall into the trap of thinking we can fix ourselves. These things aren't bad. Caring for our bodies, reading books, and meditating are all good practices, but the danger comes when we think we are the source of our own healing and peace. None of the things Granger was doing was bringing the peace he so longed for in his life.

We both struggled with the slideshow that played on a loop in our minds of River's body, lifeless and cold, his eyes rolled back in his head. It made it hard to sleep most nights, so one of the guys in the band suggested he smoke a little marijuana to relax him enough to get some rest. He invested in a weed vape pen that he would take a hit of before bed some nights. I just kind of laughed it off when I walked into a little cloud of smoke as I entered the bathroom to brush my teeth before bed. I knew he wasn't abusing anything, and he was a grieving father—my grieving husband—just wanting some reprieve. I tried it, too, a handful of times, but I didn't like the way it made me feel. So I just suffered through the sleepless evenings and visions of my darkest night.

Many of you are probably reading my story because you know our family, you know of our loss, or you may have already read Granger's book *Like a River*. In chapter 7 of that book, titled "The Dark Night of the Soul," Granger recounts in vivid detail the night he almost took his life. He was out with the guys in Boise, Idaho, one night after a show. It was a good show for them, and some of the guys were gonna go grab some drinks. Granger decided to go with them.

They walked over to the local bar, laughed, and told old stories, all while drinking more than he had since River died. When the evening wrapped up, he found himself drunkenly walking back to his tour bus alone. He details how he couldn't remember the code to the door, numbers he had pressed hundreds of times. As he fumbled for the keypad in the cold and made it inside, he realized the severity of the situation in that moment. He hadn't been drunk in a really long time. Fearing that this would cause all the emotions and pain to come flooding back, he quickly grabbed for the weed pen and took a hit, hoping it would bring him out of his drunken state a bit, but nothing changed. The slideshow kicked on and he was once again in the war of his mind.

Visions of River face down in the pool assaulted his thoughts and lies pierced his conscience that he was a failure as a father, that he had let River down. In a moment of utter despair, he fumbled for the gun he kept in the drawer by his bed for safety on the road, aiming to end the pain. You can read the story in more detail in his book, but that night my sweet, incredible husband, the wonderful father of my kids, put a cold Glock 9mm into his mouth. I cry even typing this. It breaks my heart that he felt like this was the only way out. I wish I had known. I wish I could have grabbed him, shaken him, and said, "You're a good father! I love you! We've got this! This isn't the way!"

But I didn't have to. By the sheer grace of God, Granger became aware that the voice quietly telling him to pull the trigger wasn't his own. He realized suddenly that he was under attack. He was engulfed in spiritual warfare. In that moment, he did the only thing he knew to do, crying out, "Jesus, save me! Save me, please, Jesus, save me!"

In that moment of crying out to God, the visions suddenly stopped, the gun slipped out of his hand, and he collapsed to the floor, falling asleep in a puddle of his own tears, fully clothed on the bathroom floor of his bus.

Granger texted me the next morning saying he'd had an awful night. He told me he drank way too much and came face-to-face with Satan. I asked if he got sick and he said, "Oh yeah, all night." He said the visions came and he cried and prayed Psalm 23 until he fell asleep on the floor. He never shared with me that he came so close to pulling the trigger. Not until three and a half years later.

After Granger completed writing *Like a River*, the proposal was ready from the agency, and in it was a chapter on his dark night of the soul. He knew he needed to tell me before I read about it in the book.

I was busy organizing our closet when he called me one day while he was on the road.

"Hey babe? Hey, are you where you can talk? I need to share something with you."

"Okay," I said, as I took a deep breath in.

"You okay?" He sounded serious. *What on earth could it be?* I went outside and got into the front seat of my car.

"I had a weak moment on tour a while ago."

Oh, God. Surely, he didn't have an affair. My mind was swirling.

I know Granger; I know the life of integrity he lives, just as his dad did. I trust him. I knew in my heart it couldn't have been an affair, but after all, even the best men are men at best, and I couldn't begin to guess what bomb was about to be dropped on me.

"Remember the night in Boise when I told you I met Satan?"

"Yes."

"That night, in my weakness, I pulled my gun out of my drawer and put it to my head. The visions and everything were too much, and I was ready to end it all."

I sat in my car as those words sank in. How had I not known it was that bad? And how had I not asked more questions that morning when he called me after? My mind raced, but then my thoughts were interrupted with the fact that I still had him. He didn't take his life. God spared him. *Thank you, Jesus.* I cried as he replayed the whole story. I told him how sorry I was that he was all alone and had to feel all of that and keep it a secret for so long. I told him I loved him and I was so thankful that he didn't do it. That he was still here and that it was all going to be okay. I then told him he needed to call his mom and his brothers and tell them so they could hear it from him before the world knew.

Studies show that bereaved parents, particularly fathers, are at a significantly higher risk of suicide after the loss of a child. A Danish study found that parents who lost a child had nearly double the risk of suicide compared to nonbereaved parents. The study also indicated that this risk is more pronounced in fathers, who often suppress their grief.[4]

Men are often expected to be the steady ones—the strong, unwavering protectors of their families. Society tells them to hold it together, to be the rock, even as their world crumbles around them. And so, many do exactly that. They suppress. They avoid. They bury their grief beneath layers of silence, just as Granger did. But that pain doesn't go away—it festers, leading to isolation, despair, and suicidal thoughts.

Many fathers never reach out for help, believing they should be able to carry the weight alone (remember the cable exercise at Onsite?). But grief doesn't work that way. When left unspoken, it only deepens, feeding into the feelings of shame, guilt, and an unbearable sense that they failed at their role as protector.

Grief doesn't just take an emotional toll, it's physical. Some studies show that in the first six months after losing a child, fathers experience a surge in acute illnesses, medication changes, and hospital visits.

Interestingly, studies show that while mothers often experience the sharpest pain early on, their symptoms tend to soften over time. But for many fathers, the weight of grief doesn't lift—it lingers, unspoken and unresolved, pressing heavier with each passing year. Like Granger's, it becomes a silent, relentless ache that time alone cannot heal. In one of our therapy sessions in Tennessee, our counselor asked Granger, "What is it that you want to be for your family in all of this?"

> *Grief doesn't just take an emotional toll, it's physical.*

Granger replied, "A rock, so they can all depend and rely and lean on me."

Our counselor wisely asked, "But then who does the rock lean on?" We were both silent. *Hmm. He's right.*

"I want you to think of yourself more like a tree. Strong and rooted, but able to sway and bend with the things that come your way."

Every time I read Scripture now, I always highlight the scriptures that say God is our rock. So often, men especially try to be "the rock," the strong one, but then who do they go to? Who do they lean on when life gets tough?

> The LORD is my rock, my fortress and my deliverer; my God is my rock, in whom I take refuge, my shield and the horn of my salvation, my stronghold.
> Psalm 18:2 NIV

> He only is my rock and my salvation, my fortress; I shall not be shaken.
> Psalm 62:6

For who is God, but the LORD? And who is a rock, except our God?

2 Samuel 22:32

Trust in the LORD forever, for the LORD GOD is an everlasting rock.

Isaiah 26:4

The Rock, his work is perfect, for all his ways are justice. A God of faithfulness and without iniquity, just and upright is he.

Deuteronomy 32:4

God didn't create us to be rocks. God created us as finite, fallible creatures who were made to depend solely on Him. He is the Rock. We don't have to be strong and carry the weight of it all. He invites us to lay all our burdens at His feet. He promises to be our strength. It's His power that is made perfect in our weakness (2 Corinthians 12:9).

I am not a doctor. I don't want to come at this like I know more than they do. I know PTSD is real, I know mental health struggles are real, I know there are times when people need medication for a season until they can get regulated again after trauma and loss, anxiety, or depression, but I also know we have a real Enemy out to take us down. There is one who seeks after our soul. No amount of therapy or medication or self-help is going to protect you from the one the Bible says prowls around like a roaring lion seeking someone to devour (1 Peter 5:8). The Bible urges us to remain sober-minded and watchful. The Enemy will look for any crack in your foundation to sneak his way in and attack.

Grief itself can easily become an idol, consuming us to the point that our pain becomes our identity. When we lose someone or something we love, it can be hard to focus on anything else. The memories, the loss, the "what-ifs" all cloud our thoughts. Grief is natural and necessary, but if we're not careful, it can become our everything. If I wanted to truly heal, I had to release River and shift my gaze from my son to the Giver of my son. There's a deep sense of guilt that can come with this; it feels almost like betrayal to seek healing, hope, or joy, as if moving forward dishonors the person or thing we've lost. But God showed me that there is freedom in that release. Turning my eyes to Him, trusting Him to hold my son and the broken pieces of my heart, opened the door to a peace I never thought I'd feel. The Giver, not the grief, became my foundation, and in Him I found the courage to live, love, and hope again.

The Bible tells us, "You keep him in perfect peace whose mind is stayed on you" (Isaiah 26:3). If we wanted true peace amid our grief, we needed to shift our gaze. We needed to have our eyes on Jesus. What is it that you need to surrender and release in this season the Lord has you in? Is it control over a circumstance? Is it expectation in a relationship? Is it anger or bitterness toward someone? Is it unanswered questions about pain in your life?

I want to encourage you to ask the Lord to take it from you. Ask Him to fill you with peace that only He can give. Turn to the Lord and begin to fill those spaces with His presence, His Word, and His promises. Let Him replace the weight of what you're carrying with His peace, a peace that surpasses all understanding. Trust that as you release these burdens to Him, He will sustain you, guide you, and draw you closer to His heart. True peace comes not from holding on but from opening your hands and surrendering it all to the One who holds all things together.

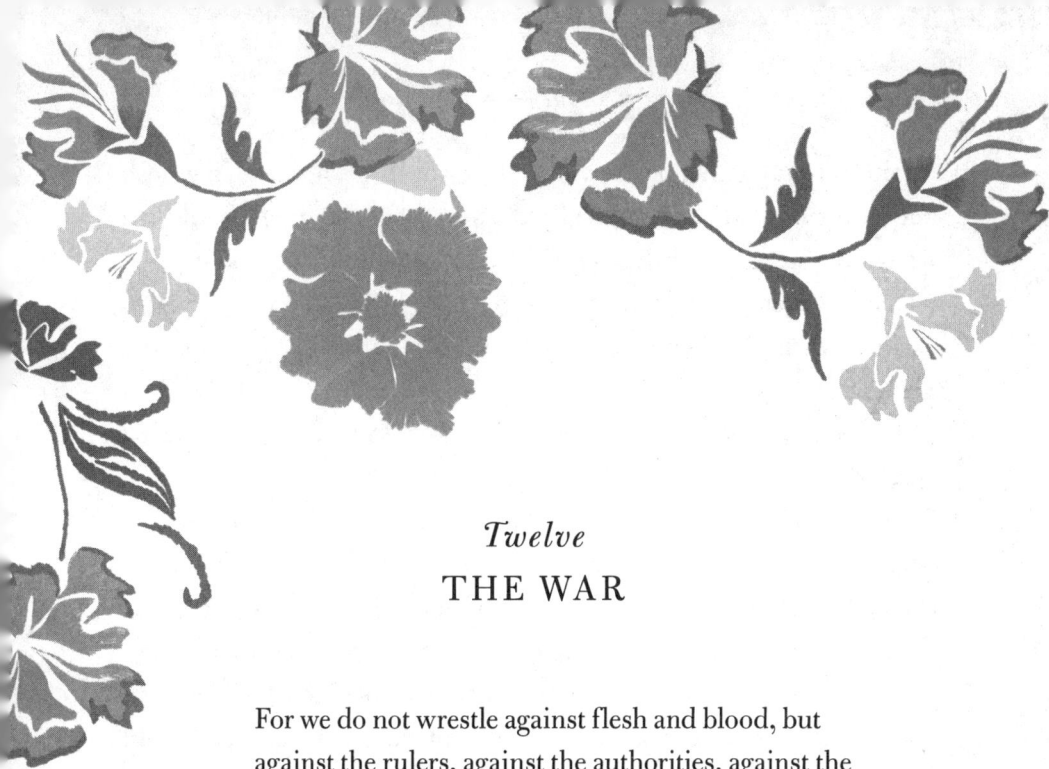

Twelve

THE WAR

> For we do not wrestle against flesh and blood, but
> against the rulers, against the authorities, against the
> cosmic powers over this present darkness, against
> the spiritual forces of evil in the heavenly places.
>
> Ephesians 6:12

There is a spiritual war raging every day in every one of our lives, but so many of us don't even realize we are in the midst of a fight. This battle isn't fought with earthly weapons or on physical battlefields but in the war zone of our hearts and minds. It's an all-out crusade for our souls, waged against our flesh, light versus dark in the brokenness of the world, and we have an enemy, our adversary the devil, who seeks to destroy us.

"The loveliest trick of the devil is to persuade you that he does not exist," wrote French poet Charles Baudelaire.[1]

Even though I felt peace when River was in the hospital, my flesh and mind were at war. Logically, I knew what the doctors told us: River had breathed for only four minutes before passing. I knew that when they turned off the machines, his little body slowly gave way to earthly death. But inside, the onslaught of doubts raged. *You didn't wait long enough. You should have prayed more. You should have held him. What kind of mother are you? You allowed your son to die. Is God really good?*

The Enemy is sneaky. He whispers lies into our minds, especially when we are vulnerable. He makes us question God's Word, His character, His power, His love, and His provision, just as he has done since Genesis 3. His goal has always been to create a wedge between us and Jesus, to make us believe we must carry the weight of this life alone. To make us believe we have more control than we do. To make us doubt that God really loves us and that He is good.

In the months after River passed, I found myself spiraling into the trap of comparison. As I mentioned earlier, I would hear stories of other children who drowned, and I would obsessively search for updates online. Would their child open their eyes? Would their child survive? Would they get to go home? My heart broke for families whose stories ended like ours, with the same heartbreaking goodbye, but occasionally I would read of a miraculous recovery, of children who, incredibly, survived without injury, making me question, *Why didn't we get our miracle? Why do they get one?* Isn't that where so many of us find ourselves when things don't go our way?

Comparison is a thief, and its target is your peace and joy.

Comparison is a thief, and its target is your peace and joy. The Enemy wants us to fixate on others' stories and to question God's goodness in our own. When our emotions are all over the place, it's easy to lose sight of what's true. We must ground ourselves in something solid and unchanging—the truth of God's Word. Feelings can overwhelm us at times, but they don't dictate truth. I love what the late pastor R. C. Sproul said: "I don't always feel His presence. But God's promises do not depend upon my feelings; they rest upon His integrity."[2]

In Scripture, God reminds us, "Fear not, for I am with you" (Isaiah 41:10), and "I am with you always, to the end of the age" (Matthew 28:20). These promises, not how we feel, are our anchor in the storm. God is with us, even when the Enemy tries to convince us otherwise.

Hagar's story, found in Genesis, demonstrates God's faithfulness and presence even when one feels so alone. Hagar was an Egyptian servant to Abraham's wife, Sarah. When Sarah was unable to have children, she took matters into her own hands and gave Hagar to Abraham as a surrogate so he could have a child. After Hagar bore a son, tension arose, and upon being mistreated by Sarah, Hagar fled into the wilderness in despair. An angel of the Lord came to her by a spring in the desert, calling her by name and assuring her that God had seen her affliction. It was there she said of the Lord who spoke to her, "You are a God of seeing. . . . Truly here I have seen him who looks after me" (Genesis 16:13). Therefore, the well was called Beer-lahai-roi, after the God who sees.

As I was writing this chapter at a local coffee shop, a young lady approached me. She had seen the cover of my laptop with my blue butterfly sticker on it. When I sat down she realized she had met me before a few years ago with her mom at a Christian conference.

"Hi, is it okay if I tell you something?"

"Of course, sit down."

Tears began to fill her eyes as she shared with me that this day was five months since the day her mom passed. She was going to go to school but decided to skip that day to buy coffee for someone else in memory of her mom. She'd planned to go to another coffee shop, but the Lord led her to this one. She saw the butterfly sticker and shared with me that it has special meaning between her and the Lord, and it was just such a sweet reminder that on a sad day, God saw her.

The Israelites experienced this too. Tired, hungry, and wandering in the wilderness, they doubted God's provision, yet He was faithful. He was always present, leading them with a cloud by day and a pillar of fire by night and providing manna, quail, and water to sustain them. Their clothes didn't wear out and their sandals didn't fail—for forty years! God never left them, even when they grumbled, doubted His care, and couldn't see what He was doing. God remained faithful.

Satan would have you believe God has abandoned you. He wants you to question how your story is turning out. He wants you to feel regret and shame and fear. But God promises He is ever present, and He is providing for you in ways you may not see right in this moment.

John 10:10 warns us, "The thief comes only to steal and kill and destroy. I came that they may have life and have it abundantly." This enemy seeks to steal our joy, kill our hope, confuse our identity, and destroy our faith and families. But when this adversary comes, God reminds us that He is the victor and we have been given the tools to fight these battles.

We can fight back with the sword of the Spirit, which is the Word of God. We can and must saturate our minds with His truth to combat the Enemy's lies. When we feel worthless, God says we are "fearfully and wonderfully made" (Psalm 139:14). When we feel unloved, God says, "I have loved you with an everlasting love" (Jeremiah 31:3). When we feel weak, God says, "My grace is sufficient for you" (2 Corinthians 12:9).

In our loss I allowed the Enemy to tell me I was a bad mother, that I had failed in the one job I had: keeping my children safe. He made me think I would never have joy again and that River's death was all our fault. He made me believe that my family would never recover and that my children's lives would be forever ruined by this tragedy. When our emotions are all over the place, it's easy to get swept up and lose sight of what's real. And the lies can hold us in bondage and shame. So we must ground ourselves in God's firm, unchanging, and reliable truth.

Your mind is free for the taking if you aren't renewing it daily. If we aren't filling our minds with the Word of God, there is room left for the Enemy to take root and fill us with doubts and lies. This isn't some red cartoon devil with horns we are dealing with. This is an accuser, a deceiver who seeks to demolish our hope, distort the truth, and destroy everything good that God has established. This is an enemy who knows the Scriptures and is after your soul for all eternity. This is someone who comes disguised as an angel of light. If we don't know the truth, we can't combat the lies when the Enemy tries to convince us that God has abandoned us, that He isn't who He says He is, that He is holding out on us.

The Enemy is after our families too—especially our children. As parents, we have a God-given duty to arm our children with the truth of His Word. Deuteronomy 6:5–9 reminds us to love the Lord with all our heart, soul, and strength and to teach His commands diligently to our children—talking about the Scriptures when we sit, walk, lie down, and rise. We can't prepare the world for our children, but we must do our best to prepare our children for the world. By grounding them, and ourselves, in God's truth, we are equipped to stand firm against the Enemy's schemes and declare with confidence, "It is written . . ." (Matthew 4:7). J. C. Ryle said, "Ignorance of Scripture is the root of all error, and makes a man helpless in the hand of the devil."[3] I didn't know the Scriptures as a young girl. And as a young woman, I allowed the Enemy to make me feel worthless. I allowed him to speak lies to me that I could never be loved or forgiven. But God says, "If we confess our sins, he is faithful and just to forgive us our sins and to cleanse us from all unrighteousness" (1 John 1:9).

Whatever you're feeling in this season of your life, there is truth in God's Word that speaks directly to it. This must be the foundation you stand on rather than what your fleeting emotions tell you. Feelings are real, yes, but they aren't always reflective of what's true. When life feels overwhelming and your heart is heavy, open your Bible. Let God's promises anchor you, reminding you that no matter how you feel, His truth is unwavering.

I remind my children often that "this too shall pass." I can't tell you how many times my kids have said, "This is the best day ever! I love my life!" and then not ten minutes later, "My life sucks, no one likes me. This is the worst day of my life."

I think of the story of Elijah in 1 Kings 19 when he said, "It is enough; now, O LORD, take away my life" (v. 4). Exhausted and overwhelmed, he fled into the wilderness and prayed to die. Elijah had had enough. He was done. But God didn't rebuke him. Instead, He sent an angel to provide food and rest. That encounter and nourishment strengthened Elijah for the journey ahead.

How many times have we felt like enough is enough? When the pains of life just keep piling up, you're already living paycheck to paycheck, and then your alternator goes out, or one of your kids needs surgery, or your dog gets sick, or someone steals your wallet, and amid all this you find out your spouse has been lying to you. You feel undone.

Elijah, like so many of us, felt like he couldn't take another step. But in that moment of deep despair, God sent an angel who gave him two things: a nap and a snack. There's something beautifully simple in that. Sometimes, when life gets too heavy and we're on the verge of breaking, all we need is a little rest and nourishment. And that's exactly what God provided for Elijah. He allowed him to sleep, then woke him up with a meal waiting. Elijah didn't even realize it, but that simple act of kindness was preparing him for the next part of his journey.

We often need the same thing. Sometimes God sends nourishment to us in the kindness of a friend providing a meal when we are sick, or in a sweet text with a verse saying they are thinking of us, or by prompting someone to come help with our laundry or pick up our kids and take them to a park for a bit so we can get some rest. There are days when life gets overwhelming, and we just need to rest. But while rest and a snack might help for the short term, we can't rely on that alone, especially when severe suffering ensues. Elijah needed more than just one meal to sustain him for what was ahead, and so do we. What he really needed was spiritual food—just like us. God told Elijah to rise and eat again because the journey was too much for him to handle on his own. The Lord sees the journey He is calling us to, and we need to be well nourished for the days ahead.

I have so many people who reach out to me, asking for a verse on depression or a verse on loss or a verse on marriage struggles. And there is power even in a single verse. I can give you a verse on just about anything, but one verse isn't enough. A single verse is like a snack. It's like grabbing a granola bar when what you really need is a home-cooked meal. Sure, it might give you a little burst of energy, but it's not going to sustain you for the long journey ahead.

God has laid out a feast for us in His Word—a whole spread full of wisdom, truth, and strength—and so many of us never even come to the table. I was guilty of this for so long. When I was reading devotionals after losing River, I was getting little bits and pieces of the Word, and those pieces gave me comfort in the moment. But when life got hard again and tears flooded me like I was back on day one, they weren't enough to sustain me. I needed more. I needed to dig into the full story, I needed to see the bigger picture of who God is and read about His plan and faithfulness.

Just like Elijah needed more than a snack to make it through the wilderness, we need more than a single verse to carry us through life. God's Word is alive, powerful, life-giving, and life-sustaining, but we have to take it in regularly, not just in crisis moments. So, rise and eat. God has prepared a table for you, a feast that will strengthen you for whatever journey lies ahead. Don't settle for an appetizer when God desires to satisfy your hunger with His feast.

But he answered, "It is written, 'Man shall not live by bread alone, but by every word that comes from the mouth of God'" (Matthew 4:4).

Living in the tension between the world and eternity, between doubt and faith, means constantly choosing to trust in God's goodness, even when everything around us seems to say otherwise. It means studying the Scriptures, equipping ourselves with the truth, so that when the Enemy strikes, we are ready. We are in a war, but we do not fight it alone. We have a Savior who has already secured the victory, who offers us life—full, abundant, and eternal. And as we navigate the battles of this fallen world, we cling to the hope that in the end, the war has already been won. So armor up and stand firm.

When Granger realized on his dark night of the soul that he was in a spiritual war, and that when he cried out the name of Jesus to save him the visions stopped, he set out to understand what had happened. Why did the visions stop when he called on Jesus? This question set him on a mission to know the Jesus he had thought he had known his entire life. Granger would have called himself a Christian. He attended church and youth camps and was baptized and confirmed in his local Methodist church, but he wasn't walking in the ways of the Lord. He wasn't living a fruitful life built on surrender to and trust in Christ. This led him on a journey of listening to sermon after sermon as he drove in his truck on the back roads of Texas. One sermon in particular changed his life. The pastor was preaching out of John 14:

> Judas (not Iscariot) said to him, "Lord, how is it that you will manifest yourself to us, and not to the world?" Jesus answered him, "If anyone loves me, he will keep my word, and my Father will love him, and we will come to him and make our home with him." (vv. 22–23)

Those words upended Granger because in that moment he knew he was loved. Right then, in his truck, on an old country back road, Granger's eyes were opened like never before and he was reborn. I thank God that we didn't lose him that cold evening in Boise. I shudder to think of what our lives would be had he taken his life that night.

One morning shortly after his rebirth in his truck, he came to me in the barn. I was sitting at the round, wooden, white table in the little living area we had created next to the RV. I had my many devotionals all laid out in front of me. Each day I would read little stories of encouragement tied to a scripture, and they would give me a little boost of hope for the day ahead (that little granola bar). I was doing okay, but I still had my moments of deep pain. Granger stopped right beside me and looked down at the table.

"Babe, I think we need to put all these devotionals away. We need to go to the Word of God. We need to read the Bible."

Looking at the spread of books and back at him, I asked, "Okay, where do we start?"

Arise and Abide

That spring, I picked up a pretty turquoise blue, floral CSB Bible and cracked open the thin pages to Matthew 1. It was the start of something new—my journey of truly studying the Scriptures and desiring to know who God really is. Day by day, I would sit and read a chapter here, a few chapters there. At first, I didn't understand much of what I was reading—so many names and stories, so much geography and history—but I kept coming back. I kept praying, asking God to reveal Himself to me, to give me understanding and strength, and to show me that there was meaning and purpose in all of this.

Slowly, my eyes started to open, and little by little, God removed the veil that had been over my eyes for all my life. Stories I'd heard before began to connect, and I saw the thread of God's sovereignty beautifully woven throughout every page. I read about so many people who God called and used mightily and how they, too, were called to seasons of wilderness, hardship, or fiery trials. I saw how God brought them through their pain, guiding them with purpose the whole way.

During those early months after losing River, I shared some of my journey on The Smiths and Instagram. I would sit in the closet, turn the camera on, and just share whatever I was feeling on that particular day. Sometimes that just meant crying and processing my grief in front of the world. My Instagram turned into a kind of diary where I poured out all my emotions day by day. People began suggesting I create a separate channel from The Smiths to detail my journey of grief, faith, and healing. At first, I didn't feel qualified to talk about pain and suffering and especially Jesus. I was still so new to it all, everything was so raw, and I was trying to find my footing as a new believer. But what I felt that day on the bathroom floor—when the Holy Spirit told me, *Enough. Seek Me.*—was so real. The call to arise, to get up, to seek Him, and to give Him glory, even through my brokenness, led me to starting *Arise with Amber.*

What began small—just me sharing a prayer or a passage from a devotional in my closet or kitchen—turned into something bigger. Soon, I found myself studying the Bible day in and day out, working on seven- to ten-page messages to bring hope to others through the pain. I shared my heart and my struggles, and people got to watch my journey in real time—the rawness of loss and the slow but steady growth of my faith as I surrendered more and more to Jesus every day. I look back at those early episodes and cringe sometimes because I was such a baby believer. I didn't always have the right words or full understanding (and trust me, even today I am still learning, still seeking, still growing), but it was real, it was honest, it was part of my journey. And my hope is that it reflects this truth: When we have a genuine desire to grow in the wisdom and knowledge of God, He is faithful to stretch us, shape us, and mature us by His grace.

And now, as I reflect on how much the Lord has done in my life, I'm thankful. I've learned so much, and the sanctification process is ongoing. There's another big church word, *sanctification*, meaning the work God does in and through us by the Holy Spirit as He molds us and shapes us to become more like Christ. This process is lifelong as He transforms us

He is faithful to stretch us, shape us, and mature us by His grace.

from the inside out. Transforming our desires to align with His will. I will never know all there is to know about Jesus, but what a joy and sweet privilege it is to study His Word. I hope people can see the slow progression of spiritual maturity that's come through the years. I am still a grieving mama, but now I am a grieving mama with a Living Hope.

"But we do not want you to be uninformed, brothers, about those who are asleep, that you may not grieve as others do who have no hope" (1 Thessalonians 4:13).

Arise with Amber has become more than just a podcast; it's a reflection of God's grace in my life, a place of healing, and a place where I can point others to the hope we find in Him.

A Wretch like Me

Something happens to you when you read the Word of God. The Scriptures tell us in Hebrews, "For the word of God is living and active, sharper than any two-edged sword, piercing to the division of soul and of spirit, of joints and of marrow, and discerning the thoughts and intentions of the heart" (4:12). God's Word has power. God's Word is life. God's Word will change you.

One day I went out to our new property to film *Arise*. It was during the time when I was still recording outside in nature, with the wind blowing and sometimes the rain falling, the dogs barking in the distance, and the wind chimes often providing the soundtrack to the message. It was usually so peaceful out there, but on this particular day I just didn't feel like I had anything in me. I didn't have the strength. I didn't have the energy. I was completely drained, emotionally and spiritually. How could I pour into others when I felt so empty inside? I tried to push through and set up the camera and lights like I did every week, but as soon as I hit Record, the tears came. I couldn't even speak. I just sat there, staring at the camera, sobbing, unable to force the words out. So I packed everything up, put it back in the car, and sat in the driver's seat. Then it all came pouring out.

I sobbed—loud, uncontrollable sobs. I was grieving for River, but then something shifted in my heart. All the sadness I had been carrying for Riv turned into a deep, soul-wrenching cry of repentance. In that moment, sitting in my car, I was hit with the weight of my sin. I went from crying "I am so sorry, River!" to "I am so sorry, Lord, I am so, so sorry!" It felt like a tidal wave of guilt and shame, things I had buried deep inside for years rising to the surface. I cried out to Jesus, begging for His forgiveness. My heart broke as I realized how much I had sinned against a holy God.

I used to pray before bed every night asking for forgiveness for things I had done, but it was almost repetitive and routine, not really evoking any emotion. I felt bad for past "mistakes," as I used to call them, but this time it was different. Every sin I could remember came flooding back. I confessed awful sins from my teens and twenties and went as far back as I could, to my childhood, confessing things I had long forgotten—lies I told, things I stole. I ransacked my memory, trying to lay it all bare before the Lord. I begged Him through tears to forgive me. I wept at the realization of how sinful I had been, how depraved my heart was. Those weren't just mistakes I had made, those were sins against a holy God, against the One who gave His life for me. Against a Savior who was pure and blameless. And He loved me enough to still choose me. That is truly amazing grace.

The realization hit me like a freight train—He died for all of it. Every single sin I was confessing, He carried it and it was nailed to the cross. And in that moment, I wasn't just sad or remorseful; I was crushed. This was godly sorrow, the kind of sorrow that makes you see yourself for what you truly are—a wretch in need of grace. I must have sat in that car crying for the better part of an hour.

"The sacrifices of God are a broken spirit; a broken and contrite heart, O God, you will not despise" (Psalm 51:17).

But here's the beautiful, unbelievable, undeserving part: When we come to Jesus, when we confess our sins, when we repent and trust in the finished work of Christ, no matter what we have said or done, we are not just forgiven; Scripture tells us He remembers our sins no more.

Think about that. As humans, we may say we forgive someone, but honestly, most of us still hold on to things, we still hold a grudge, and the next time they mess up, we're quick to remind them of all their past wrongs. Not so with God. His forgiveness is complete, absolute. Ugh. It breaks me.

Hebrews reminds us of this truth: "For I will forgive their wickedness and will remember their sins no more" (Hebrews 8:12 NIV). Jesus, our High Priest, didn't just offer Himself as a sacrifice, He became the sacrifice—the perfect, spotless Lamb. But He also mediates a new covenant for us, a covenant built on a better promise. A promise that doesn't condemn us but sets us free. He doesn't hold our sins over our heads, waiting to remind us of how we've failed time and time again. He doesn't keep a record of wrongs as so many of us do. No, when we come to Him, He wipes them away completely, as though they never even existed. He washes us white as snow. We are cleansed by the precious blood of Jesus.

We deserve none of this. We deserve the full weight of God's wrath. We deserve death, hell, and eternal separation from Him. But Jesus took it all. Every ounce of punishment that was meant for us, He willingly bore. He stepped down from glory, leaving the perfection of heaven to enter into His creation. He lived the perfect, sinless life that we could never live. He was mocked and beaten, and His bloodied body was nailed to a cross—for you and for me, for our sin. The King of kings, the Lord of lords, hung on a tree, His flesh torn, His blood spilled. There has never been, nor will there ever be, a greater love.

But that wasn't the end of the story. On the third day, He rose, proving that He was the once-for-all atoning sacrifice and substitute for our sin. He conquered death, hell, and the grave. And for those of us who turn from our sin, who lay it all at His feet and trust in Him as Lord over our lives, we're not only forgiven—we're welcomed into the family of God, adopted as sons and daughters of the Most High! Hallelujah!

> But to all who did receive him, who believed in his name, he gave the right to become children of God, who were born, not of blood nor of the will of the flesh nor of the will of man, but of God.
>
> John 1:12–13

> Even as he chose us in him before the foundation of the world, that we should be holy and blameless before him. In love he predestined us for adoption to himself as sons through Jesus Christ, according to the purpose of his will.
>
> Ephesians 1:4–5

Can you believe that? The good news of the gospel isn't just that our sins are wiped away but that we are adopted into His family. That is incredible news, the best news for sinners like you and me!

You may feel abandoned. You may feel unloved or forgotten. You may not have a "good" earthly mother or father. You may have been abused or mistreated by those who were supposed to protect you. I am so sorry for what you may have had to endure. But though our earthly families can let us down, our heavenly Father will not. You may not have an earthly parent, but you have a Father. A good, good Father who welcomes you into His family, who invites you to share in His inheritance forever. His arms are wide open for you, friend.

Sister, brother, if you are carrying the weight of past sin—if guilt and shame are suffocating you, dragging you down—call it what it is and take it to the cross. Jesus has already taken it for you. You don't have to live under that bondage any longer. The Enemy loves to whisper lies, doesn't he? He'll tell you that God could never forgive you, that you've gone too far, that you're too broken, too stained, too damaged, too far gone. But he's a liar. Don't insult the grace of God by staying stuck in that lie.

When we refuse to forgive ourselves and cling to our past mistakes, it's like telling Jesus, "Your sacrifice, Your blood, wasn't enough to cover this." But His sacrifice was more than enough to cover your every stain. Every sin—past, present, and future—was nailed to that cross. The price has been paid in full. Don't let the Enemy deceive you into holding on to what Jesus already took care of.

But friend, when you realize this incredible truth and turn to God, don't ever look back. Don't turn around to pick up those old chains of sin and shame. Colossians 3:9–10 tells us, "Do not lie to one another, seeing that you have put off the old self with its practices and have put on the new self, which is being renewed in knowledge after the image of its creator." Don't put on that old self again. Leave it behind and run hard after Christ. Keep your eyes forward, fixed on Him, and don't let anything pull you back to what you've been set free from.

In that moment in my car, when I was crying out to Him, I finally understood. I didn't just ask for forgiveness—I felt the weight of His mercy and grace wash over me. My sin was so heavy, but His grace was greater. He had already carried every bit of it to the cross, and in His mercy, He lifted it off me. He untangled the lies from my mind. And He will do the same for you. Come and see.

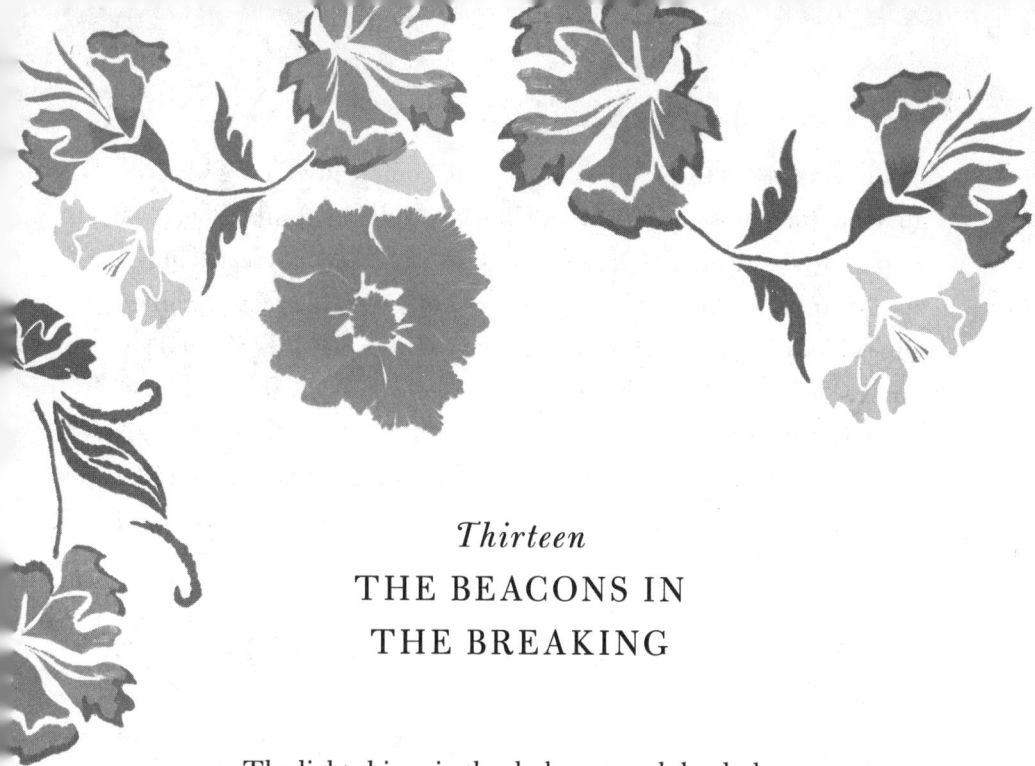

Thirteen

THE BEACONS IN
THE BREAKING

The light shines in the darkness, and the darkness
has not overcome it.

John 1:5

Spring has always been my favorite time of year. There's just something about watching new life emerge from what seemed barren and dead. The bright greens, the colorful flowers and butterflies—everything feels fresh, like the earth itself is breathing hope back into the world. Spring always reminds me of River. He used to pick yellow dandelions for me, those little flowers most people see as useless weeds. Many people don't realize that dandelions are more than just weeds. They're packed with medicinal qualities—more vitamin A than spinach and more vitamin C than tomatoes. It's amazing to me that something so often overlooked or even stepped on is filled with so much goodness.

I think about that a lot—the care and complexity God gives even to something as small as a dandelion. And then I think about how much more intricately He's woven us together. You were created in His image, knit together in your mother's womb at the perfect appointed time and with such specific detail, from your DNA to the gifts and talents He's given you. It's mind-blowing when you really think about it. He has seen your life from beginning to end. He knows your joys, your sins, your sorrows, and He knows what it will take to bring you into His arms. From birth He is molding and shaping us into the image of His Son by the careful refining, pruning, preparing, and transforming work of His hands.

This season of my life, the one where everything felt so dark and barren, was one of the most transformative times I've ever experienced. When River died, I had said that a part of me—the girl I used to be—died with him. But through that death and the ashes of that grief, through surrendering and seeking Jesus, something new emerged. I blossomed into a different version of myself, one I never could have imagined, one who sees the world and the Lord more clearly. One who loves deeper and experiences true joy and peace in Him. One who desires to do what pleases God. One who wants to share the good news of Jesus with the world.

I mentioned that River used to pick yellow dandelions for me. But we also loved blowing the feathery, parachute-like structure, known as pappus, into the wind. We called them "wishers." Now, in order for the white seedling puff of a dandelion to develop, the yellow flower must die. Jesus said in John 12:24, "Truly, truly, I say to you, unless a grain of wheat falls into the earth and dies, it remains alone; but if it dies, it bears much fruit."

Only when I died to myself—died to my sins, died to my flesh—was I able to come alive in Christ. Only then was I able to bear fruit by the power of the Holy Spirit's work in me. He caused my dead heart to come alive. "Therefore, if anyone is in Christ, he is a new creation.

The old has passed away; behold, the new has come" (2 Corinthians 5:17).

It wasn't until after River died that God truly awakened my soul—and Granger's too. In losing the life we had known, we were brought into a deeper need and longing for God.

God knows exactly what it will take to bring each of us into His arms. For some, He draws us gently through the faithful teaching of parents or pastors in our childhood, or maybe it happened for you at a youth retreat, or maybe your moment was one like Granger's. Maybe God awakened your heart while you were driving down a back road after a devastating loss.

Through the pain and brokenness of losing River, I've come to see how God's faithfulness shines brightest in the darkest places. His grace has carried me in ways I never imagined, but His faithfulness isn't just for me—it extends to those I've cried out to Him for. One of the most personal examples of this has been watching God redeem my little brother Colin's story.

God's faithfulness shines brightest in the darkest places.

For nearly two decades, I prayed for him. I spent so many nights on the bathroom floor, pleading with God to rescue him from the grip of addiction. Sometimes I felt helpless, knowing I couldn't save him. But God, in His perfect timing, answered in a way only He could.

On January 2, 2022, Colin found himself in a dark hotel on the bathroom floor crying out to God to save him. He couldn't take any more of the life he was living. He surrendered it to God and reached out for help. Today, my brother is three years sober, a believer in Christ, married to a wonderful woman, thriving in a good job, and a member of a healthy church. God's faithfulness is undeniable in his life, and he's begun to share his story of grace and redemption with others. His story, like mine, is a powerful reminder that no one is too far gone for God to reach and that our prayers truly matter. Don't give up hope. Don't stop praying.

If I were to ask each person reading this book, I would guess that you probably didn't come to know Jesus in the mountaintop moments of your life. No, if you've experienced a deep, personal relationship with Christ, it's likely that He met you in the valley, in the depths, on the bathroom floor. When the world around you felt like it was closing in, when you were brought to your knees in surrender, and when you finally reached the end of yourself, that's when you discovered the beginning of His strength.

God loves us far too much to leave us where we are.

God loves us far too much to leave us where we are, and sometimes that means He allows our hearts to break so He can heal them. "Come, let us return to the Lord; for he has torn us, that he may heal us; he has struck us down, and he will bind us up" (Hosea 6:1).

As Samuel Rutherford, a seventeenth-century Scottish pastor, once said, "God is too wise and too skilled a physician to afflict His people for nothing. He can use your very wounds to heal you."[1]

If God didn't love us, He wouldn't entrust us with these pains. Isaiah 41:10 reassures us, "Fear not, for I am with you; be not dismayed, for I am your God; I will strengthen you, I will help you, I will uphold you with my righteous right hand." It's in those broken places, those moments of utter despair, that His grace becomes our lifeline.

If we never experienced pain or suffering, we would never recognize our deep need for our Savior. Without the reality of sickness, we wouldn't fully appreciate the gift of health. Without the experience of darkness, how could we ever truly revel in the glory of the light? Though the fall of man brought deep brokenness into the world, it opened the way for us to experience the depth of God's incredible redemption and His unrelenting love for His creation. It's in the valleys, those moments of deep struggle and loss, where we find Him most intimately. When we are stripped of all we think we can rely on, forced to let go of our own strength, we learn to lean entirely on His mercy and grace.

True transformation happens in these moments, when we come to the end of ourselves and realize that we have nothing left but Him. It's in this brokenness that God often does His greatest work, revealing His power in our weakness. As 2 Corinthians 12:9 says, "My grace is sufficient for you, for my power is made perfect in weakness."

If we never experienced pain or suffering, we would never recognize our deep need for our Savior.

In the valleys, when all else fades away, we see Him for who He truly is—our Healer, our Hope, our Rock and Redeemer, and the One who carries us through. This is where true growth happens, where endurance is built and where the deepest change in us takes root.

In our pride, we become so self-centered, always focused on what we want and when we want it. We fall into a trap of believing a me-centered gospel—one where our personal comfort and desires take center stage. We build up our little kingdoms here, consumed with our own worldly lives and material possessions, and lose sight of the bigger picture. But the truth is, this life isn't about our comfort. It's about being conformed to the image of Christ. And Christ suffered. If God didn't spare His only Son, why would we think we would get out of this life unscathed?

Jesus Himself didn't walk an easy path. His life was marked by servanthood, humility, and ultimate surrender to the Father. He endured mocking, relentless testing, betrayal by those closest to Him, and eventually murder on a cross. Romans 8:17 says, "And if children, then heirs—heirs of God and fellow heirs with Christ, provided we suffer with him in order that we may also be glorified with him." If Jesus, the perfect Son of God, faced such deep sorrows, why do we think our paths would be free of hardship? His life is our blueprint, and through our trials, we are being shaped and purified into His likeness. It's in the pain, in the wilderness, that we begin to understand the depth of His love for us and the power of His ultimate sacrifice.

As British pastor and author Charles Spurgeon said,

> Rest assured, if you are a child of God, you will be no stranger to the rod. Sooner or later, every bar of gold must pass through the fire. Fear not, but rather rejoice that such fruitful times are in store for you, for in them you will be weaned from earth and made meet for heaven; you will be delivered from clinging to the present and made to long for those eternal things which are so soon to be revealed to you.[2]

Just like the dandelion breaks and spreads to sow new life, the brokenness in our lives created something new—not just in us but in others. Our story, River's story, became a seed that God used to reach people we never would have known. Through our vulnerability, we spurred others to begin opening their Bibles again, searching for Jesus, reconnecting with their faith. These were blessings in the breaking—new life sprouting from the darkest moments.

When people come to us and say, "Because of your story I've found my faith again" or "Because of your son, I opened my Bible and started going to church," I am thankful, but I know it wasn't River who did it. I know it wasn't anything I did. It was all by the grace of the Lord, and if He used us as a vessel in some way to shine His light, then I am humbled and honored to be a small part of His plan.

We see this breaking and blessing all throughout Scripture. When Jesus broke the bread and fish, it fed a multitude (Matthew 14:19). When the woman broke the jar of nard and poured it on Jesus' feet, it was a sweet blessing, an anointing for His burial (Mark 14:3–9). The pressing of grapes and olives produced wine and oil (Job 24:11). And ultimately, the greatest breaking of all—Jesus' broken body for you and me—brings about healing, salvation, and eternal life to all who would believe.

It is so hard to see the blessings when you are in the middle of the brokenness. But when I look back with fresh eyes—eyes with an eternal perspective—and a heart of surrender, I see just how much good has come from our loss. We've met some of the most incredible people on this grief journey, forging new lifelong friendships with brothers and sisters in Christ, people we wouldn't have known without the hurt.

Two people were given a chance for life through River's organ donation. His life and death led to the creation of the River Kelly Fund, a nonprofit established in his honor that now helps many people in need. Granger and I travel the country sharing about hope and the good news of our risen King. River's little life became the catalyst for so much good. Even in the breaking, even when life feels barren and hopeless, God is at work. He sees you. And just like the dandelion and spring after the cold, new life will come. It may not look like what you expected, but the beauty and blessing that come from the breaking can sometimes give way to something even more beautiful than you could have ever imagined.

As Oswald Chambers said, "If through a broken heart God can bring His purposes to pass in the world, then thank Him for breaking your heart."[3] I have now come to a place where I can thank God for that breaking because it brought me to Him. My supreme treasure. The greatest gift of all. Jesus.

I think of a story I heard recently—it's a simple story but one that perfectly illustrates this idea of being broken for a purpose. A woman was in Dollar Tree one night, standing in line behind a mom with two kids. The older child had a pack of glow sticks, and the toddler was screaming for one. The mom opened the pack and handed the toddler a glow stick, and he was happy just walking around with it. But then the older boy took it, and the toddler started screaming again. Just as the mom was about to step in, the older child bent the glow stick and gave it back, and suddenly the toddler noticed it was glowing. The older brother said, "I had to break it so that you could see the full effect." The woman listening felt God speaking to her in that moment: "I had to break you to show you why I created you. You had to go through it so you could fulfill your purpose."

That toddler was perfectly happy with an unbroken glow stick, just swinging it around in the air. He didn't understand what it was made to do—until it was broken.

Just like that little boy with his unbroken glow stick, I was perfectly happy in my seemingly happy little life, in my home with my good marriage and my happy children, before River died. But I wasn't walking in the fullness of God's light. I wasn't living out the purpose He had called me to. I was doing nothing for His kingdom. I may have felt alive, but I was still dead in my sins. I believe with all my heart that God is sovereign, and nothing happens outside of His control. River's death was not a senseless accident, nor was it a punishment. While I don't fully understand His purposes, I trust that God in His infinite knowledge allowed this heartbreaking event and has used it to transform me. It wasn't until I was broken that God lit a fire in me for Jesus, for repentance, for the gospel, and for others who are suffering. Only a God as powerful and loving as ours could bring redemption and purpose out of such loss.

I pray that God doesn't break your heart to bring you to Him, but if He does, I pray you can learn to thank Him for it. There is purpose in that breaking, friend. And if you're in that place right now, hold on. God is working. Surrender and seek Him in the middle of the hurt. I can promise you that new light and new life will emerge.

Fourteen

THE RACE

Let us run with endurance the race that is set
before us, looking to Jesus, the founder and
perfecter of our faith.

Hebrews 12:1–2

I spoke in an earlier chapter about the thief of joy and my battle with
comparison. A few weeks after we buried River, I took London and
Lincoln to an ice cream shop in the little square downtown. As we
sat there, I noticed a middle-aged dad with his toddler on his shoulders, laughing and carefree. Suddenly, I was mad. Why did he still
have his little boy when we didn't? I didn't know this man, but in that
moment, I envied him and I was angry. Grief does that to you. It makes
you wrestle with the unfairness of it all—why others get to keep what
you've lost, why their life seems so much easier and yours looks like a
dumpster fire. It's so common in our human nature to look at everyone
around us and compare our lives to theirs.

Proverbs 14:30 reminds us, "A tranquil heart gives life to the flesh, but envy makes the bones rot." In that moment, I was only seeing what I lacked, and that comparison stole my peace. I wasn't able to fully enjoy the time with my two beautiful, healthy children because my heart was consumed with what had been taken from me.

It's easy to look at the lives of those around us and wonder, *Why do they have it easier? Why don't they have to face the same struggles I do? Why does she have healthy kids and my child is suffering? Why do they have the big house and the fancy car, while we're barely making ends meet?*

In John 21:22 Jesus said to Peter, "If it is my will that he remain until I come, what is that to you? You follow me!" The Christian life is often compared to a race. We are told in Hebrews to "run with endurance the race that is set before us" (12:1). Jesus was reminding Peter that he needn't worry about John. He should be focused on his own path and race toward Jesus.

I've never been one who enjoys running. I was that girl in middle school who faked cramps to get out of running cross-country. I've tried to love it, tried to reach that elusive "runner's high" that people talk about, but it never happened for me. Sprinting, sure, I can do that. But long-distance running? No, thank you. It's exhausting and painful—just like life sometimes. And maybe that's why it's such a fitting analogy for our walk with Jesus. Running the race set before us isn't easy. It takes discipline, focus, perseverance, faith, and, most of all, trust.

But we aren't running around aimlessly in circles. And we aren't running to prizes and trophies that will tarnish and fade. We run for an eternal crown—a reward that will never perish. As Christians, we are running with direction, toward a finish line where we get to spend eternity with our Creator in the new heaven and new earth. And that is a prize worth running for.

Paul reminded us in 1 Corinthians 9:24, "Do you not know that in a race all the runners run, but only one receives the prize? So run that you may obtain it." This race we're running has eternal significance. From the day we are born, we are set on a path toward eternity, where we will spend it in one of two places: in fellowship with Jesus or separated from Him. The stakes are high. How are you running? Are your eyes on your lane or someone else's? Are you even running at all? Or are you just coasting through this life like I was before the Lord lit a fire under me?

This is one of the hardest races we will endure. From the moment we enter this world, the deck is stacked against us because of Adam and Eve and the fall. We are born into sin, into a broken world where things are not as they should be. We don't get to choose our starting point—where or when we are born, our family, our circumstances, or the challenges we'll face. Yet, in His wisdom, God has set a unique race before each of us. He has equipped us with specific giftings, challenges, blessings, and, yes, even sufferings. But He hasn't left us to figure it out on our own. He's given us tools—His Word, His Spirit, His people, and His promises—to run this race well. But we have a choice: Will we follow His blueprint or will we try to run our own race, our own way, comparing hardships on the journey?

Running a race takes endurance. Hebrews 12:1 tells us, "Therefore, since we are surrounded by so great a cloud of witnesses, let us also lay aside every weight, and sin which clings so closely, and let us run with endurance the race that is set before us." But how do we do this? How do we keep running when life gets hard, when the race feels too long or too painful, when we physically feel like we can't take another step?

First, we must prepare. Just as athletes train with discipline and consistency, so must we. I knew the battle I would face each day. I knew the Enemy would attack my mind if I left space for it, so I made sure to prepare by spending time with the Lord before I stepped out into the world. I prayed and read my Bible, asking the Lord to guard my heart and thoughts and help me to keep my eyes on Him.

I would repeat Scripture to myself anytime I started feeling sad or looking in someone else's direction. We can't run effectively if we are weighed down by distractions and entangled by sin. Hebrews 12:1 reminds us to "lay aside" or "throw off" (NIV) everything that hinders us so that we can run freely. What is hindering you in your race today? Is it unforgiveness, is it addiction, is it fear? Is it distraction or comparison?

Second, we must remember that we are not running alone. I was contacted by a woman in Tennessee after River passed away. Nicole had lost her son, Levi, to drowning just the year before. She comforted me in my pain and gave space for all that I was feeling. But she also encouraged me that it would get better. That this pain can lighten. When so many others were saying "Oh, year two is brutal. It's worse than year one," she would say, "It doesn't have to be. Everyone's journey is different. It still hurts but it does get lighter." Our families are forever connected by the loss of two precious little boys, and I'm so thankful for that friendship that emerged from hardship.

Notice that Hebrews 12:1 begins by reminding us we are surrounded by a great cloud of witnesses. Our ancestors in the faith have run this race before us, and their stories encourage us to keep going when life gets hard. We have not only the stories in Scripture to spur us on but also the stories and testimonies of so many around us encouraging us that we, too, can make it to the finish line. If you are in a good local church, praise God! If you have been encouraged by other believers in your life, thank Him! Those are gifts He has given you to help in your race.

Third, we must remember that preparation isn't always easy. Just like any kind of training, it can be painful. I told you I don't like to run, but I do enjoy lifting weights. One day, I was working out with an app on my phone, and the trainer (Sagi from Beach Body, if you're wondering) was pushing me through a final set of military presses. My muscles were burning, my shoulders felt like they couldn't handle another rep, and I wanted to drop the weight. But right in the middle of the struggle, he yelled, "Keep going! You've got to enjoy it. Why? Because it's only pain—that's it. Pain will go away, and you'll say goodbye to it. You want to dance with it, you want to hug it, because then the pain drives you! Keep going!" Just as physical pain can drive us to grow stronger in training, tearing and shaping our muscles, the pain we endure in life can drive us closer to Christ. Pain, though temporary, shapes us and changes us if we allow it. It teaches us to rely on God's strength and to keep running the race He's set before us.

Finally, we aren't told to just run the race. We are told to fix our eyes on Christ while doing so. Hebrews 12:2 encourages us to look "to Jesus, the founder and perfecter of our faith, who for the joy that was set before him endured the cross, despising the shame, and is seated at the right hand of the throne of God." When we focus on Jesus, we remember that God has a purpose for our race, even in the darkest valleys. He knows exactly what we need to reach the finish line, and He walks with us every step of the way.

Acts 14:22 reminds us that "through many tribulations we must enter the kingdom of God." Jesus never promised an easy race, but we are promised the greatest companion of all while we run and an incredible inheritance that awaits us just over the hill.

John Newton, the English pastor and writer of the hymn "Amazing Grace," once told a story about a carriage during one of his sermons. He said,

> Suppose a man was going to New York to take possession of a large estate, . . . and his carriage should break down a mile before he got to the city, . . . which obliged him to walk the rest of the way; what a fool we should think him if we saw him wringing his hands and blubbering out during the remaining mile, "My carriage is broken! My carriage is broken!"[1]

Two hundred years later, pastor John Piper added to this story in one of his messages:

Sometimes your kid falls over the cliff when the wheel comes off the carriage, and you fall out of the carriage and crush your knee so that you never walk normal again on the mile that's left in your life. That happens. So, I don't want to make light of broken carriages here.

We all can laugh at a broken carriage, but it's not as easy to say, "I lost my kid when he was five of Leukemia." I've buried so many kids. You know this. There are whole sections of Wood Lawn Cemetery with little teeny places reserved, and to watch a dad carry a white box is a carriage that you don't make light when it's broken.

But he can know, for himself, for this child, for his wife: "Just a mile, just a mile over the hill I get the child, I get the wife, I get the health, I get the world, I get God, I get a new body to enjoy it all." And that's how his tears will not be the tears of those who have no hope. He will weep. We will weep—though we won't weep as those who don't have an inheritance.[2]

The Lord has really been ministering to me through Psalm 23. How He is our Good Shepherd. The psalmist wrote,

> The LORD is my shepherd; I shall not want.
>> He makes me lie down in green pastures.
> He leads me beside still waters.
>> He restores my soul.
> He leads me in paths of righteousness
>> for his name's sake.
> Even though I walk through the valley of the shadow of
>> death,
>> I will fear no evil,
> for you are with me;

> your rod and your staff,
>> they comfort me.
> You prepare a table before me
>> in the presence of my enemies;
> you anoint my head with oil;
>> my cup overflows.
> Surely goodness and mercy shall follow me
>> all the days of my life,
> and I shall dwell in the house of the LORD
>> forever.

My eyes have really been opened to the fact that God, in His loving-kindness, has marked out a specific path for each of us. He leads us in paths of righteousness, and He also leads us on a path through the valley of the shadow of death. Both of them are paths marked out by God. And because He is good, both paths are good, though they may not feel good at the time.

Our Shepherd leads us, walks with us, and pursues us all the days of our lives. He provides, nurtures, restores, and prepares a place for us. We just have to keep our eyes on Him, trusting that He will lead us through.

No matter how your race has unfolded, no matter how hard your path has been or will be, look to the One who promises to bring you through the valley.

David Gibson wrote, "It may not yet be part of your theological framework that all things, including each valley, come from God's fatherly hand, but it needs to be. For if God is not in charge of the valley, how do you know he can get you through it?"[3]

This road will not be easy, but I can promise you if you endure to the end it will be worth it. As Piper said, just over the hill, you get your child, you get your health, you get your spouse, and you get the healthy body back. But greatest of all, you get eternity with Jesus.

Not only that, but we rejoice in our sufferings, knowing that suffering produces endurance, and endurance produces character, and character produces hope, and hope does not put us to shame, because God's love has been poured into our hearts through the Holy Spirit who has been given to us. (Romans 5:3–5)

So, we cry out to God in our distress, we pray for strength to persevere, and we do not lose heart. We press on until we hear Him say, "Well done, good and faithful servant." Those are words I long to hear when I cross the finish line of this race of a Christian life. Even when my carriage breaks and I must crawl, even if I am knocked down again and again, I am determined to fight the good fight, keep the faith, and finish my race. Are you with me?

AFTER

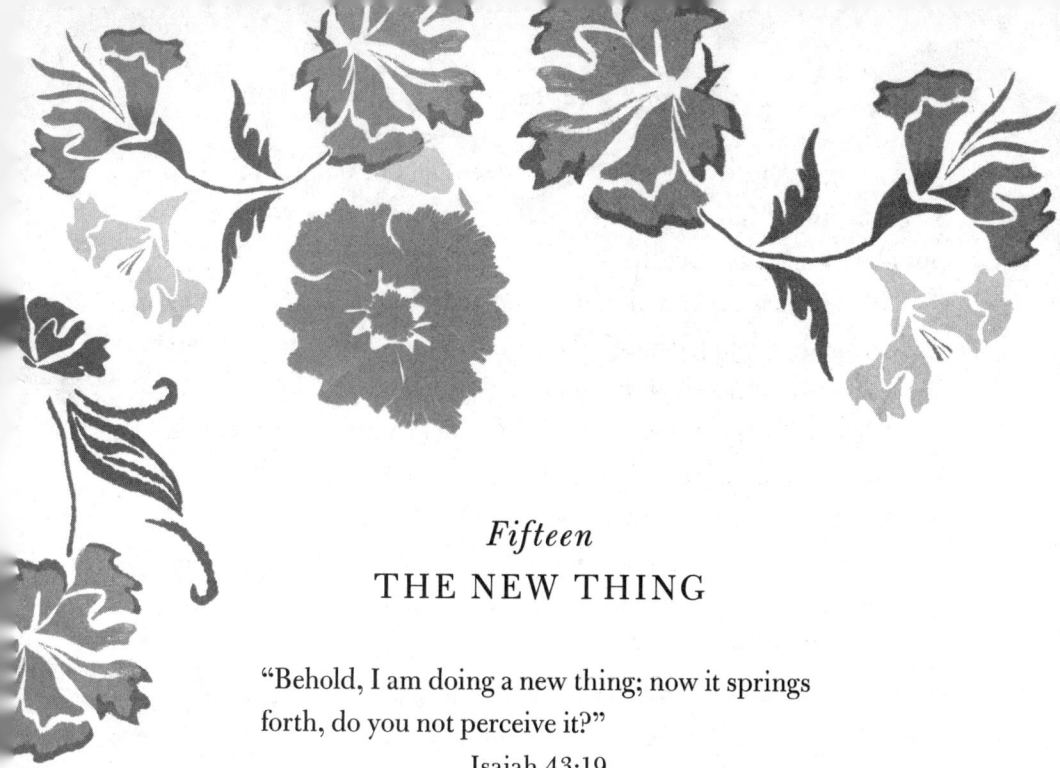

Fifteen

THE NEW THING

"Behold, I am doing a new thing; now it springs
forth, do you not perceive it?"
Isaiah 43:19

Behind the scenes of all that was going on during our mourning and healing process, something new was stirring. Around this time in the winter of 2019, I was in the bathroom of the new home getting ready for the day, when Granger came in and leaned casually against the counter and posed a question that caught me completely off guard.

"Hey, do you think you would ever want to try for another baby?" he asked, his voice gentle but filled with a sense of longing.

I froze, my heart seeming to stop beating in that moment. How could we even think about another child when we had just buried our baby? Everything was still so raw.

"No, absolutely not," I responded, my voice firm and seemingly sure. "I couldn't do that. It would feel almost like a betrayal to River, babe."

Granger nodded, respecting my feelings but not entirely letting go of the idea. "I just wanted to put it out there in case you were ever possibly thinking about it."

The discussion ended and we moved on in our new routine of walking with the limp of grief. We went through the motions of parenting and work, still carrying the heavy burden of loss. But the idea of another child kept resurfacing, and Granger said, "I just feel like I have so much more love to give." It was something he couldn't shake, a feeling he believed the Lord had placed on his heart.

I was torn between my pride, my sadness, and the nagging thought, *If the Lord wants us to have another baby, why hasn't He placed it on my heart?* One night, lying in bed, I prayed, *Lord, if it is in Your will for us to have another baby, can You show me something, confirm it through someone else, or guide me in this path?*

I remembered a conversation with my mother-in-love, Debbee. Her husband, Chris, wanted to leave their home in Dallas after their son Tyler graduated from high school. Chris was retired and he loved his ranch. He had the idea of moving their youngest son, Parker, to a smaller school away from the big city. But Debbee was content where they were and didn't want to move until Parker would graduate years later. Then one day as Chris was plowing at their ranch on his tractor, he told Debbee that the Lord had whispered to him to move there. Debbee laughed, thinking he was kidding, and said, "Are you sure that's not your own voice you're hearing?" But he was confident in what he felt, so being the praying woman that she is, she went to the Lord for discernment and guidance and peace.

She felt God remind her that He doesn't speak only to her. That He speaks through others and, yes, that includes her husband. Even though in her flesh she didn't want to move there at that time in their life, she stepped out in faith and trusted where the Lord and her husband were leading. She realized she didn't have to be fully on board with it just yet; she just needed to let go and trust.

That memory softened my heart and made me see that God doesn't have to speak only to me. I came to Granger a few days later and said, "If this is something you feel strongly about, then I should honor that. Let's see what our options are." I still didn't feel ready. I didn't know if I ever would, but something in me led me to explore it.

As I mentioned earlier, we had been so sure that our family was complete with three children that I had opted for a tubal ligation after River was born via cesarean. On New Year's Day 2020, I messaged my ob-gyn:

Hi there! Hope you are doing well! Granger has been talking about another baby, and we were discussing my tubal. Was the tubal we did reversible, or no? We don't even know for sure if we would try to have one if it was reversible, but if it's not, it would answer a lot of the unknown questions we have. Thank you so much, and I hope you had a wonderful new year! Amber.

A few days later, on January 6, I received a reply:

Good morning! Sorry for the delay. I was out of the office last week. Yes, the type of tubal ligation that was performed is technically reversible, but the most successful approach would be IVF. I would discuss with your insurance to see if a tubal reversal is covered. Some choose reversal because it is overall less expensive (if covered), but IVF is more successful generally. I would start out with a consultation with an REI (infertility) doctor to gain the most information.

We wrestled with this decision, weighed down by the sadness of missing River and the options before us, both of which were expensive and uncertain. I didn't know much about IVF, only that it helped couples struggling with infertility. I justified it by thinking, *I never had an issue getting pregnant before, my tubes are just blocked now.*

Surely, this would be okay. But I couldn't dismiss the feeling that we were playing God in some way. Then again, hadn't we played God when we decided to get my tubes tied in the first place? Knowing what I know now, I wouldn't recommend a tubal ligation or a vasectomy for anyone. Life is unpredictable, and despite our best-laid plans, we have no idea what will happen. We can make all the plans in the world, but it is the Lord's purpose that will stand. In the words of Isaiah regarding the Lord, "Declaring the end from the beginning and from ancient times things not yet done, saying, 'My counsel shall stand, and I will accomplish all my purpose'" (Isaiah 46:10).

After much wrestling and prayer, we decided to pursue IVF. We were still new believers at this point, unaware of the challenges and ethical dilemmas we would face. In my naivete, I thought, *God has gifted these doctors with the skills to help people build families. God is the One who opens or closes a womb. We would only be planting a seed. It would be up to the Lord whether He allowed it to grow. What could be wrong with that?* Looking back now, I see the complexities and potential pitfalls of IVF, and I can't say that I would counsel a friend in that direction if they came to me asking for advice. But at the time it seemed like a viable path that the Lord was leading us on, and, as a sweet friend recently reminded us, we were doing the best we could with what we knew at the time.

We found a clinic in Austin, and I met with the doctors. After discussing my history, the doctor cautioned that at my age, the percentage I would conceive and carry a pregnancy to term was low, but there was still a chance.

I started the multiple hormone shots and oral medication. I'll never forget the first shot I gave myself. I'm not afraid of needles, but this was terrifying. I was scared of messing up the dosage or injecting the medicine into the wrong spot. After a few days, I got the hang of it, but my lower abdomen was covered in tender bruises for weeks from the multiple daily injections. The hormones affected my hair, making it brittle and dry, a side effect I hadn't anticipated, and one medicine gave me a terrible rash all over my torso. The IVF process was filled with shots, blood tests, sonograms, shedding tears, and constant questioning if we were making the right decision.

After I was sedated for the egg retrieval, they managed to retrieve fourteen eggs. In the end, of those, only two were viable—both male. When I read the results, I cried. Was this God's plan for us? Was River really meant to be with us for only three years? Was this sinful? Were we always meant to have another child? All these emotions were overwhelming to say the least.

We kept the IVF process from the kids, not wanting to share any news until, God willing, we were pregnant. We didn't want to get their hopes up only to be dashed. Just as we received the retrieval results, the world shut down in March due to COVID-19. All fertility treatments and procedures were put on hold. Schools closed, Granger's touring stopped, and we found ourselves with unexpected time to simply be together as a family. In that quiet time, we reflected on our journey, prayed a lot, drew closer to the Lord by reading our Bibles each day, and began to trust that whatever the outcome, God would sustain us through it.

Still not feeling settled in our new house, Granger would search real estate apps looking for a place to call home. The same month COVID hit and we got the results from the egg retrieval, Granger found a place he thought was perfect. It was about twenty miles away from where we were, and it sat on ten acres. On the land were two barns and a windmill, something Granger had always wanted. He drove out one day and called me to come meet him.

As I pulled up, I got out of the car and stepped into the most gorgeous field of wildflowers. Flowers that River used to pick me all the time. Yellow dandelions and Indian paintbrushes and bluebonnets. It really looked like a Slaughter painting in real life. W. A. Slaughter was a Texas-based artist who became famous for painting bluebonnets and Texas Hill Country scenes. Granger's parents had one, as did my grandmother. It was the one thing I wanted as a reminder of her when she passed, and my aunt Chrissie was kind enough to allow me to have it. It's even more special now because while I was writing this book, my sweet aunt passed away from a sudden heart attack.

"What do you think?" Granger asked.

"It's beautiful, but there's no house."

"See that barn over there? Hear me out. What if we rent an RV and live in it on the property while we build our home?"

I paused for a moment, seeing the concealed excitement behind his eyes, and said, "I love it—let's do it!"

If I had learned anything over the past ten months, it was that tomorrow isn't promised. We're meant to live fully and appreciate our time together. I used to carefully weigh big decisions, but at this stage in my healing, I realized I didn't want to think and wait so long that I'd miss opportunities and adventures with my family. Life's experiences are here for us to embrace, and we shouldn't hold back when they come our way. I'm not encouraging anyone to make silly decisions that could hurt you or your family, but this was an opportunity for a fresh start, and I wanted to embrace it.

There was so much change during that time. The loss of River, moving homes, COVID shutting down touring and a lot of the world, our children changing schools. Now we were about to move into an RV in a barn right before the Texas summer while going through IVF treatments.

It almost didn't happen, though. We called the Realtor while we were at the property and asked if we could talk with them about buying the land. The Realtor said, "Oh, we are taking that off the market with all the COVID stuff happening."

"But what if we pay full price?" Granger asked.

Thankfully they took the offer, and we were off to the races. Now we just needed a builder and a place to live in the meantime.

We reached out to friends and cold-called companies to see if anyone would let us borrow an RV while we built our house in exchange for sharing the company on our YouTube channel. Explore USA loved the idea, and within a few months they were driving a big fifth wheel into the large metal barn on the property. The kiddos loved it. They still say it was their favorite house to date. It had a small back bedroom where Granger and I slept, a nice kitchen area with recliners and a small kitchen table, then another back area where the kids slept, with bunks and closet space. We set up our TV and couches right outside the RV in the barn itself and tried to make it as homey as possible. The four of us got really close in that camper. We endured the scorching heat; all the roly-polies, scorpions, and wolf spiders; and the "ice-pocalypse" that froze most of the state of Texas and crushed almost every tree on our land.

The Dream

That spring on a beautiful April morning, Lincoln came into the bathroom where I was getting ready for the day. He had just woken up; his hair was still messy and undone. He hugged me and said, "Mommy, I had a dream and River was with me."

"Aw, sweetie, he was? What was your dream about?"

When he told me, I was in such shock I had to grab my phone to record what he was saying. I went and got Granger so Lincoln could relay the dream to him, and when he began telling it, I hit Record. This is verbatim from the voice recording:

> He told us about heaven. He said he had fun with Sue [a giant T. rex we had seen at a museum recently], he said Jesus was fun and the third part was in my dream, Mama was having a baby but we didn't know it yet, and River was playing with our baby brother. It was a boy. But he told us that and then we knew.

And then he said, "Did you see me by the pool?" And he woke up from CPR. And then we moved back to the old house and then we swam for a wittle bit and then we went to go feed Murray [the sweet goat next door]. Because that was his favorite thing. And then I was sad when I woke up.

How in the world? Things like this don't make sense. The kids didn't have any idea we were trying for another baby. I had lots of messages during this time on Instagram of other people dreaming I was pregnant with a boy as well. I tucked all that away and wondered, *Will God really grant us another baby?*

Trusting in the Hand You Cannot See

We still kept IVF a secret from the kids, but the phone rang in June, and we were told the clinic was reopening. We were able to schedule our first embryo transfer for July 8. I remember the day clearly. The procedure was quick, meticulous, and routine. They checked my vitals and handed me the standard hospital gown and those cozy socks they give you to ward off the cold. I lay back as I put on the hair net, and they wheeled me into the room. The doctor confirmed my name and checked my numbers on her chart. I leaned back, taking a deep breath as she prepared for the transfer.

The nurse walked in, carefully holding the needle that carried our microscopic embryo. She inserted it into my uterus, double-checked its placement, and transferred our baby into my womb. Now we could only wait, our hearts filled with anticipation, praying that this tiny new life would implant and grow, but we knew it was all in God's hands. I had done all I could to prepare my body and my heart for this new life. I went in for my blood work about ten days later to confirm if I was pregnant.

Then the call came. July 17. It was a hot summer day in the barn.

I remember we were all sweating from the heat. My heart raced as I ran to grab Granger, pulling him inside the barn from his yardwork. We perched on top of the stone table in the little living room we had created, side by side, and I answered the phone on speaker.

"Hello?"

"Hi, Amber," the voice on the other end began, warm and familiar. "We have some good news for you. Your hCG levels came back really high—they're at 262. It looks perfect. So, you're definitely pregnant. That's a really good, high number. Congratulations!"

I couldn't speak. My eyes welled with tears. This was happening. All that we had prayed for was coming to fruition. Maybe we really *could* have joy again.

"Thank you," I finally managed to say, my voice choked with emotion. "I'm sorry, I'm crying . . . thank you so much." I hung up and turned to Granger. We embraced, the tears flowing from us both. My gosh, we were pregnant with another little boy. *Thank you, Lord.*

The first week of August came, and with it my first ultrasound. The doctor moved the probe around, her eyes focused on the screen. But as she continued, her expression changed. The warmth in the room dimmed like the lights.

"Hmm, I'm not seeing the growth I'd like to see," she said gently. "I want you to prepare for a possible miscarriage. But it's still early, so come back next week, and we'll check again."

I left the clinic feeling defeated. But I knew, deep down, that this was not in our hands. It was in the Lord's. Granger and I prayed boldly for our little boy, hoping that he was just hiding, that the doctor hadn't gotten a clear look.

A week later, we returned, hopeful but nervous. The probe moved again, and this time I saw it—the tiny flicker of a heartbeat on the screen.

"There he is!" the doctor said.

Tears filled my eyes once more. What a roller coaster these months had been—the grief, the joy, the uncertainty, the constant back-and-forth. It was almost too much.

As I approached nine weeks, it was time for my graduation appointment from the IVF facility. This would be my last visit before transitioning to my ob-gyn for the remainder of the pregnancy. Granger couldn't be with me (he was preparing to head out on tour), but I wasn't alone. The nurses, who had become a sweet support system over these months, greeted me with cheers and smiles. They knew all that our family had been through over the last year.

"Today's the day! We're so happy for you!" they exclaimed, their joy infectious.

"Thank you all so much," I said, smiling and hugging them tightly. "I'm going to miss you guys."

I took off my clothes and lay under the sheet one last time, lying back on the table, eyes fixed on the screen above. The doctor dimmed the lights and began the ultrasound. I watched the screen, waiting to see my baby, waiting for that little flicker of life. But the probe moved slowly—too slowly. The doctor's silence grew heavy. Her lips pressed together.

Our eyes met, and I knew.

"Oh, Amber, I am so sorry," she said, her voice filled with sympathy. "There is no longer a heartbeat. We don't know why this happens sometimes. I'm so sorry."

"Okay," I whispered, my voice barely audible. "It's okay." I sat up, the sheet still draped over me, and swung my legs over the side of the table.

"There are a few options," she continued, her tone quiet and gentle. "We can schedule a D&C, I can give you medication, or you can go home and let the miscarriage happen naturally in a few days."

"I'll go home," I replied, feeling numb.

"Do you have someone you can talk to about this? Are you going to be okay?" she asked, concern evident in her eyes.

"Yes," I assured her, mustering a small smile. "I'll be okay."

I had already survived the worst thing I could ever imagine. I was pretty sure I could handle anything now.

The doctor and nurse left the room, giving me a moment alone. I got dressed slowly, the heaviness of what had just happened settling over me. As I left the clinic, I hugged the nurses again, tracing my fingers along the tiny colorful footprints of babies painted on the wall. Each step felt burdened as I walked to the elevator, the reality of loss sinking in, yet again.

As I walked out of the clinic and got into my car, the tears I had been holding back finally spilled over. I fumbled for my phone, texting Granger with trembling hands to let him know I was coming to see him before he left town.

When I pulled up to the farm, he walked toward me. I just shook my head and he knew. He wrapped his arms around me, and we hugged in silence, my face in his neck. Granger didn't cry; I think we were both just worn out and confused. How could this happen? Why would God guide us to try for another baby, only to take it away before it could even fully develop? Why did Granger feel so strongly that we were meant to have another baby, and what was behind that dream Lincoln had?

Four days later, on a quiet Sunday morning around 11 a.m., the miscarriage began. I felt the first cramps and knew what was coming. I looked up and whispered, "Okay, Lord. I trust You." It was what I had learned to do—trust Him in the midst of pain, even when I didn't understand. I entered the one bathroom we all shared in the barn, remaining there in intense pain, on and off the toilet and lying on towels spread across the concrete floor for the next several hours. I cried and prayed but lifted this pain to the Lord.

The next morning, I woke up feeling drained, utterly exhausted but at peace. I wasn't sad or angry. I just felt hollow. Granger, back from tour at this point, seeing what I was going through in the weeks that followed—the numbness, the continued bleeding, the back-and-forth to the doctor to make sure everything had passed—felt a sense of guilt. He came to me and said, "We don't have to do this. I don't want you in pain anymore. We can stop."

But I knew, despite everything, that we couldn't stop. I was confident in the way the Lord was leading us. We had one embryo left, and we couldn't just leave it frozen in a lab, suspended in time. We had already decided that we would go through only one cycle of IVF. If it was God's will for us to have this baby, we would. If not, then we would know that our journey to have another biological child after River was not meant to be.

The miscarriage left me bleeding and cramping for three weeks, each day a painful reminder of the loss. Eventually, I had to return to the doctor for a procedure to remove a polyp they found in my uterus. My body took a few months to heal, the physical pain gradually subsiding, but the emotional wounds lingered. If you are in a place of still feeling the ache of sorrow or loss, I understand. While we may heal physically, the body keeps the score. The body, heart, and mind remember. We learn to walk with a hidden disability, so to speak. We carry the pain with us as we try to move forward. God sees you and doesn't expect you to carry the weight on your own. Psalm 55:22 says, "Cast your burden on the LORD, and he will sustain you; he will never permit the righteous to be moved."

As we prepared for the final embryo transfer, I made a decision: I didn't want to go through the hormone shots again. I wanted to do this as naturally as possible, even though the entire process of IVF felt anything but natural. To me, skipping the medication felt like the most honest way to approach this last attempt, trusting fully in the Lord to allow this baby to implant and grow, or not.

On December 8, my mom's birthday, we went in for our final transfer. The procedure was the same as before, the same routine, the same waiting. And then, mid-December, we got the call—we were pregnant again. Wow. *God, You are so kind.* I wanted to guard my heart, to not let hope swell too quickly after everything we had been through. But despite my fears, I allowed myself to feel the excitement for this new blessing, knowing that this baby was in God's sovereign hands and trusting that whatever happened would be His will for us.

Sixteen
THE MAVERICK

Every good gift and every perfect gift is from above,
coming down from the Father of lights, with whom
there is no variation or shadow due to change.

James 1:17

I knew from the moment we were trying to get pregnant again that I wanted this new baby to have the letters of River's name somewhere in it. I ran through options, and there weren't many. We discussed Oliver and Averitt. And if it was a girl we decided on Everleigh. But Maverick was the sure winner by a landslide. One, it's just a really tough, cool name. Two, *Top Gun* is one of Granger's favorite movies. I love it too. And three, Maverick refers to an unbranded calf, symbolizing someone who tends to wander and doesn't follow the crowd. The term came from Samuel Maverick, a nineteenth-century Texas rancher who chose not to brand his cattle, and it later became associated with someone who is a free spirit or someone who makes their own path. And boy does this name fit.

My pregnancy with Maverick was a beautiful chapter in my life, filled with joy and quiet anticipation. I typically hold back when I talk about my pregnancies because I know how difficult they can be for many women, but I was blessed with wonderful experiences each time. I loved being pregnant, watching my belly grow and feeling little kicks and turns inside. I never dealt with nausea or sickness, and aside from some major swelling with London toward the end, pregnancy was a breeze for me. Maverick's pregnancy was no different until the last three weeks.

Granger mentioned once that he thought I didn't fully allow myself to love and embrace this pregnancy like I had with the others, at least not until I held Maverick in my arms on the day he was born. I didn't realize it at the time, but maybe, deep down, I was trying to protect my heart from more pain. After all we'd been through, it's possible I was subconsciously guarding myself, just in case.

I made it all the way through the pandemic without getting sick, but a few weeks before Maverick was due, I came down with COVID. It was brutal. I've never experienced a cough like that in my life—deep, relentless, and exhausting. My whole body ached, and I coughed day and night, so much that my throat became raw and sometimes bled. It takes a lot to bring me down—if you're a mama, you know we don't get to rest when we're sick. But this time, I physically couldn't get out of bed for three weeks. I worried constantly, thinking all that coughing might dislodge Maverick somehow, and I was terrified they might take him away from me after delivery to keep him safe from the virus.

When the day finally came, August 20, 2021, I still tested positive, but the doctors assured me it was common with that strain to test positive for weeks after. We drove to the same hospital where all our babies had been born. The familiarity of it brought a mix of emotions—nostalgia, anxiety, hope. We made our way to the maternity ward and pressed the call button to enter.

"Good morning, can I help you?" the voice asked over the intercom.

"Good morning, I'm here to have a baby," I replied, my heart fluttering with excitement and nerves.

"All right!" came the cheerful response.

I watched as Granger put on his scrubs one more time—the hair net, the shoe covers. I couldn't believe this was happening again. I could always sense his nervousness each time in those moments right before I was to deliver. On a day that most people would describe as the best day of their lives, Granger always said it was one of his worst. Each time he had to sit helplessly as I was prepped for surgery and watch as his wife was cut open, organs exposed on the table. Everything was out of his control, and all he could do was pray, waiting for the moment when our baby would take their first breath and make their first cry and when I would be put back together.

As they wheeled me back, the nurse asked, "What type of music would you like?" I never really cared about the music. I always said, "Whatever you want to listen to." But that day, Granger chimed in, "Whatever keeps your hands steady."

The procedure began, and as they pulled little Maverick into the world, Garth Brooks's "The Dance" played softly in the background:

> *I could have missed the pain*
> *But I'd have had to miss the dance.*[1]

Tears streamed down my face as I heard Maverick's first sweet cry. I was a mama again—something I hadn't expected but something God had known all along. As I lay there, humbled by God's goodness, I realized this chapter of my life, though unplanned by me, was exactly what my heart had been longing for. God's plan, full of grace and mystery, was far better than anything I could have envisioned. Holding sweet Maverick in my arms, I felt the tender reminder that even through the uncertainty and pain, God was bringing new life and joy into my story in ways I never thought possible.

Maverick brought so much joy back to our aching hearts, a new light in our darkest days. But his arrival didn't make the grief disappear. In those early weeks, I would often find myself nursing him, tears streaming down my cheeks as I rocked him gently in his nursery. I was overflowing with gratitude for the blessing he was, but the ache for River lingered, still ever present, just below the surface. It was a really confusing thing to think that if we didn't lose River, we wouldn't have Mav. Now, people will say, "God could have given you Mav if He wanted to," and He most certainly could have, but my tubes were tied and we were done, so short of a miraculous conception it just wouldn't be true. Those crazy postpartum hormones didn't help my grief-and-joy situation either. I was a total hot mess.

One day, my mom peeked into Maverick's room as I nursed and saw my sorrow mixed with love as tears streamed down my face. She simply hugged me and said, "I'm so sorry; I love you." It was one of those moments where words couldn't fix anything, but her presence meant everything. One of the hardest things for my mom—and I've heard this from other parents too—is feeling so helpless when watching your child go through grief. You want to take away their pain, but you can't. It was incredibly difficult for her to watch us suffer over the last few years, while she was also grieving in her own way over the loss of her grandson.

Grief and joy can beautifully coexist.

I've learned that grief and joy can beautifully coexist. They don't have to compete for space in our hearts; we can welcome them both at the same time. So, I would rock and nurse and cry and smile. I allowed myself to feel it all.

The kids adored Mav from the moment they laid eyes on him.

They would wake up early and excited before school just to hold him, their faces lighting up with pure love. Lincoln, especially, couldn't get enough of his baby brother. There were times when I had just gotten Maverick to sleep, and I had to gently keep Lincoln at bay because all he wanted to do was slather him with kisses and hugs.

We faced criticism from some who suggested that we were trying to replace our son. But nothing could be further from the truth. Maverick—or any baby born after loss—is never a replacement. He is a beautiful new chapter in the grand story that God is writing in our lives. Maverick was always meant to be here. He has a purpose that is uniquely his. God had him in His plan all along, even if we didn't know it in our limited understanding of this fleeting life.

Maverick's presence didn't erase our pain, but it brought a new kind of healing—a reminder that life, even after loss, can be beautiful again. His life is a testament to God's faithfulness, showing us that even when we're deeply wounded, joy can find its way back into our hearts, blossoming right alongside the grief.

I know what some of you may be thinking. *I didn't get my happy ending, Amber. I'm still in the thick of it. I'm still on the bathroom floor. I didn't get a new baby to love. I didn't get the redemption you found.* I hear you, and my heart aches for you. I know there are some of you who are still navigating those painful days, wondering why God hasn't brought the restoration or redemption you've been praying for—the new job, the spouse, the child you long for, the healing you so desperately need.

I've seen the heartache of women who have endured multiple miscarriages after a loss, and I hurt for them too. I don't deserve Maverick. I don't deserve anything. I can't explain why God works the way He does, and I don't have all the answers. But what I have learned, through my own journey, is that His ways are higher, even when we can't see it. In His infinite love for you, He knows the plans He has for you, and He knows the timing. Trust in Him through it all, even when it's hard.

God is a God of restoration. But I also know that for some, that restoration might not come on this side of heaven. It's a hard truth, but it's one I've had to grapple with myself. Sometimes, the restoration we long for is something we won't fully experience until the life to come. But I want to assure you that it *will* come. The brokenness we endure now—the pain that feels endless—will all be made right in eternity.

His Word reminds us in 1 Peter 5:10 that "after you have suffered a little while, the God of all grace, who has called you to his eternal glory in Christ, will himself restore, confirm, strengthen, and establish you."

Scripture also assures us that our suffering is not meaningless. In 2 Corinthians 4:17, Paul wrote, "For this light momentary affliction is preparing for us an eternal weight of glory beyond all comparison." What we suffer now, as heavy as it may feel at times, is light compared to the eternal glory that is being produced in us. Every tear, every heartache, every moment of pain is shaping us, refining us, preparing us for a glory that will be revealed in eternity. Romans 8:18 echoes this, saying, "For I consider that the sufferings of this present time are not worth comparing with the glory that is to be revealed to us."

It's okay to feel the way you do. It's okay to wrestle with the questions, the doubts, the pain. But it's not okay or healthy to stay stuck there. Don't set up camp in the valley that God intends to bring you through.

Even though I walk through the valley of the shadow of death, I will fear no evil, for you are with me; your rod and your staff, they comfort me. (Psalm 23:4)

I want to encourage you to trust that Jesus is with you, right there on the bathroom floor. He doesn't need an invitation. He is already present, in every painful place; even when you can't see how things will ever get better, trust that He knows. He longs to be with us in our suffering, and for those in Christ, He promises that we are never alone.

I don't say this lightly or as a cliché; I say it as someone who has walked through deep valleys and has truly seen and tasted that the Lord is good. He is the Good Shepherd. He leads His flock through every valley, every trial, every test, every wilderness season, every fiery furnace of affliction. He is the One who not only knows our path but designed it for us with the intent of bringing us closer to Himself and, ultimately, welcoming us home. But the sheep must follow the Shepherd. Peace, hope, and joy are not going to magically fall into your lap. Look to Jesus, the Prince of Peace, our Living Hope, and our Source of Joy.

I am not asking for any more pain to come into my life, but I will tell you those early days, weeks, months, and even years of my grief were the closest I have ever felt to Jesus. I still desire Him now, I still love to read His Word, but by His grace He has healed so much of my heart to the point that I miss the days I truly clung to and depended on Him just to have the strength to do the next thing. There is something about the gritty rawness of deep pain where He truly reveals that He is so close to the brokenhearted.

I once saw a quote that said, "We learn facts about Jesus in Sunday school, but we get to know our Savior deeply through the gift of suffering." The deepest lessons aren't learned in comfort, they're forged in the fiery trials. The seminary of suffering teaches us more about who God is and who we are than an easy life ever could. You are not alone or forgotten in this season the Lord has brought you into. And I'm praying that you find comfort in the One who holds you close, even in the darkest of times. Trusting Him doesn't mean the pain disappears, but it means you're not carrying it alone. And it means that whether in this life or the next, He will restore what has been lost.

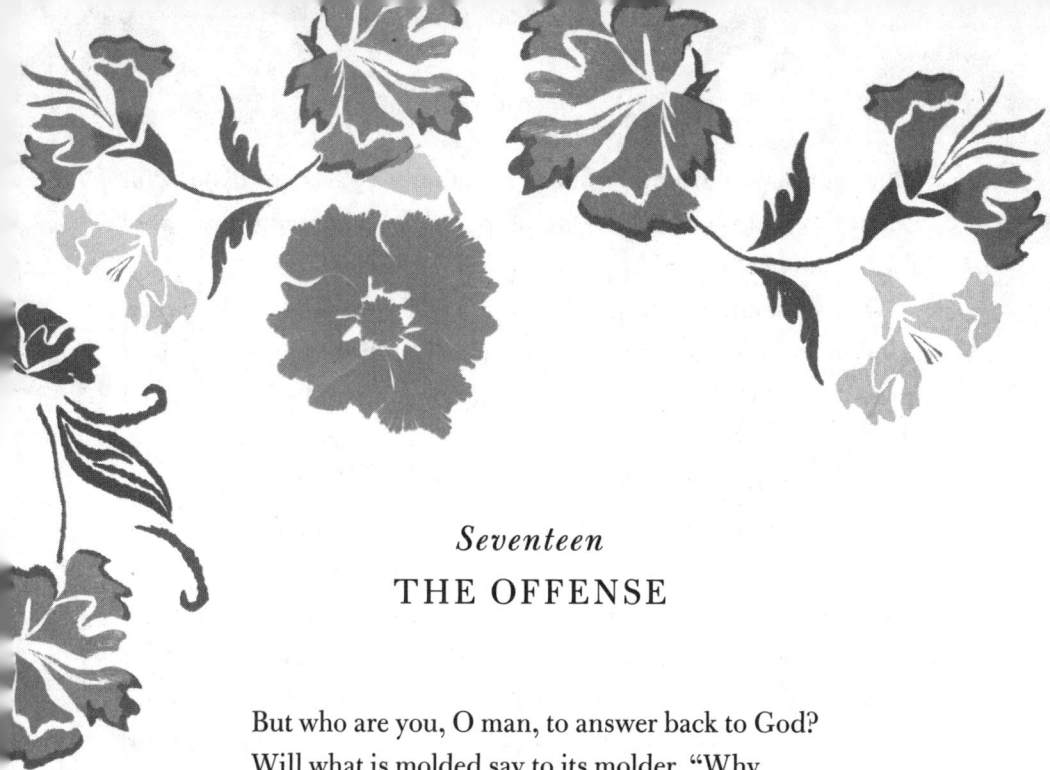

Seventeen
THE OFFENSE

But who are you, O man, to answer back to God?
Will what is molded say to its molder, "Why
have you made me like this?" Has the potter no
right over the clay, to make out of the same lump
one vessel for honorable use and another for
dishonorable use?

Romans 9:20–21

I don't know where you are in your own journey through suffering.
You might be on day one of pain and sorrow, feeling so broken you
can't see past the tears. Or you may just be starting to find your
footing again after a season of heartache. Or you might have been
suffering for twenty-plus years and still can't seem to find the joy that
everyone speaks of. Maybe you haven't experienced severe sorrow

yet but you have a friend or family member who has, and you want to help them, or you want to be prepared for when your season of suffering comes.

You might know Jesus and have been walking with Him for years. Or you might be a brand-new believer still finding your way around and wrestling with lots of theological questions. Maybe you don't believe any of this and can't understand the Christian walk.

I want to hold space for wherever you are right here, right now, especially if you're in the thick of your lowest season. When I was on day one of my loss, I didn't want to hear all the platitudes that God had a plan or that He just needed another angel. I didn't want to hear that God gives His hardest battles to His toughest soldiers or that He was working it all out for my good. You see, only two of the above statements are even true, but I still didn't want to hear it. I just wanted my son back. I just wanted my pain to end and my life to go back to the way it was.

On the other side of the coin, people would tell us that God had nothing to do with our son's death. They would say, "God would never take a child or cause suffering. He just wants you to be happy" or "It was all Satan, but what the Enemy meant for evil, God will turn and use for good."

That didn't make me feel better either. If God had nothing to do with it, then where was He? Was He not as powerful as everyone says He is? Does He not care? Is He not in control? Does Satan really have the upper hand?

I want to acknowledge that sometimes, especially in the beginning, it's okay to sit in the suck. It's okay to not say a word. It's okay to feel all that you are feeling—the confusion, the anger, the sadness. Let the tears fall. Grieve your loss. Cry out to God. Yell and scream if you must. But there comes a point in your journey when you do need to hear truth. And as your sister in Christ, having seen the goodness of God, having read His Word and seen how urgent and transformative and life-giving it is, I have to tell you these things you are about to read.

There comes a time when we have to get out of our feelings and get in the Word of God. We have to take our eyes off of ourselves and fix our eyes on Him. So many struggle in grief because they don't know the God of the Bible. We have such a small view of our Creator that when the hard things of life come, we think He isn't big enough for our pain. We will never trust someone we don't know, especially with the hard pieces in our story. So how can we trust God if we don't know Him? The only way we are going to grow in our trust in the Lord is if we shake the dust off our Bibles and read them. We must decide what we believe about God, His character, and His holiness before suffering hits or we will crumble like sand when the storms rage and the waves crash against us.

My transformation came when I began studying the Scriptures. When I prayed for God to open my eyes to His truth, I started to clearly see the goodness of God on every page. I began to see His character and read about His sovereignty in every story.

Genesis 50:20 doesn't say that God merely turns around what Satan or man intended for evil. It says that God *meant* it for good. From the very beginning, God had a purpose in Joseph's story. He rules over both the good and the painful. Scripture is clear on the sovereignty of God over and over again. We read verses like these:

> Who has spoken and it came to pass, unless the Lord has commanded it? Is it not from the mouth of the Most High that good and bad come?
>
> Lamentations 3:37–38

> "I form light and create darkness; I make well-being and create calamity; I am the LORD, who does all these things."
>
> Isaiah 45:7

"See now that I, even I, am he, and there is no god beside
me; I kill and I make alive; I wound and I heal; and there is
none that can deliver out of my hand."

Deuteronomy 32:39

These verses might be unsettling to some, but for the Christian,
they bring comfort! They reveal a picture of an all-powerful God who
is not distant from our suffering but ever present in it! They reveal a
picture of our good and faithful Lord having everything together in the
palm of His hand when everything around us seems to be falling apart.
Every tear, every trial, every sorrow is within His purpose, part of a
much larger plan that our finite minds just can't grasp. Throughout
Scripture, we see men and women brought through immense pain, only
to discover that God was working something far greater behind the
scenes.

Look no further than Job's story. God didn't merely allow Satan to
test Job—He offered him up on a silver platter. "Have you considered
my servant Job?" God asked in Job 1:8. He knew the trials that lay
ahead for Job. He gave Satan permission to take everything Job held
dear—his livestock, his servants, even his ten children (yes, ten). And
yet, in the face of this unimaginable loss, we read that he uttered these
words: "Naked I came from my mother's womb, and naked shall I
return. The LORD gave, and the LORD has taken away; blessed be the
name of the LORD" (Job 1:21).

Job tore his clothes and shaved his head in grief, but he still
praised God.

I will say I did not praise God on day one of my suffering, and I
can bet you didn't either. What faith Job had!

But if that wasn't enough, Satan returned to God, and this time,
God allowed him to afflict Job's very body. Painful boils covered him
from head to toe, and yet, even as Job sat in ashes, literally scraping
his sores with broken pottery (um, ouch!), he refused to curse God.

His wife, broken and bitter as one would be, urged him to throw in the towel, to curse God and die. But Job's response hit me to my core when I read it: "You speak as one of the foolish women would speak. Shall we receive good from God, and shall we not receive evil?" (Job 2:10).

It's a question we all must wrestle with. Why is it that we seem to accept only the good things from the Lord? Can we learn to accept that both the blessings and the suffering come from the same nail-scarred hands that bled for us? Because that's what the Bible teaches.

> In the day of prosperity be joyful, and in the day of adversity consider: God has made the one as well as the other, so that man may not find out anything that will be after him. (Ecclesiastes 7:14)

God, in His boundless wisdom, either ordains or allows both joy and sorrow for His glorious purpose. And this is something that we can't come to know and believe if we aren't spending time in the Word of God. This comes from the Holy Spirit leading us in the way of truth.

I always found it interesting that the Enemy took all Job had but left him his wife. The Enemy knew that leaving her would test Job's faith even further. She was a voice of doubt, urging him to turn away from God. He's a crafty one, that Satan. But Job stood firm, trusting in the Lord even when nothing made sense. Can we, like Job, come to a place of worshiping in the dust, even if? Even if our marriage feels like it's falling apart, even if our health never gets better, even if our child walks away from the faith, even if we bury our baby or our prayers seem to go unanswered for so long, even if life doesn't look like we thought it would?

"Though he slay me, yet I will trust in him" (Job 13:15 KJV). Will you? There is so much weight in the small words of Scripture—words like "but" and "yet." My prayer is that you come to a place where you can lament honestly, cry out to the Lord, bring your sorrows to Him, but still remember His goodness. That you would say, "Yet, I will trust in You." It's in those sacred spaces of lament, in the but and the yet, where pain meets promise. It's where faith rises in the midst of suffering. Where we call to mind all that God has done, trust in all He still will do, and choose to walk by faith and not by sight.

The Bible tells us that "all Scripture is God-breathed and is useful for teaching, rebuking, correcting and training in righteousness, so that the servant of God may be thoroughly equipped for every good work" (2 Timothy 3:16–17). These stories, like Job's, are here to teach us, to equip us for the hard paths we will face. God has given us these testimonies to remind us that suffering is not meaningless. It is not always a punishment for the "bad" or a reward withheld from the "good." Pain, suffering, and wilderness seasons happen to the righteous, the faithful, even the ones who have been serving the Lord for decades.

Job's story shows us that even in the deepest suffering, God's purpose prevails. We don't always see it in the moment (sometimes we never fully do), but He is always working, always moving for His glory, and what seems like chaos to us is still within His perfect control and timing.

And through it all, we can trust that He is good, even when life hurts. Because in the end, God is not just trying to make us happy; He's making us holy. God, in His vast love for you, cares more about your holiness and sanctification, your heart posture toward Him and your address in eternity, than He cares about your comfort in this vapor of a life.

How Small We Are

I am in awe of the way the Lord designed our bodies, our minds, our very lives. It's breathtaking when you pause and think about it. The intricate design of men and women's bodies, perfectly crafted to fit together to create life. The way our senses allow us to experience the world around us—how we can taste the sweetness of a ripe strawberry or the explosion of flavors in a great Italian meal, how we can see the vast spectrum of colors in a sunset over the ocean, or feel the warmth of a loved one's touch. God didn't have to create the world this way. He could have made it all bland and colorless, and we wouldn't have known the difference.

Then there is His delicate yet intentional detail in how He gifts each of us with specific talents. I sit in awe that He cares so much for us. I mean, who are we?

> When I look at your heavens, the work of your fingers, the moon and
> the stars, which you have set in place, what is man that you are mind-
> ful of him, and the son of man that you care for him? (Psalm 8:3–4)

You may be a mother or caregiver with the gift of patience, able to soothe and comfort a crying baby or elderly parent at all hours of the night, pouring love and security into those tender moments. Or perhaps you have the gift of hospitality and are able to create beautiful, warm, and welcoming spaces for others, making them feel valued and right at home.

Maybe you're a teacher, uniquely gifted not only in teaching but also in boosting confidence in your students, nurturing not just minds but hearts. Sometimes giving your students the care and attention they are lacking at home. Perhaps you're incredibly skilled at organizing (that's you, London!) or leading teams with vision and integrity in the workplace, fostering environments where others can thrive.

God may have blessed you with a heart of compassion, being the first one to reach out and comfort a friend in need, send a kind text, or deliver warm cookies and a fantastic meal. Or maybe He's given you the creative ability to paint or sing (the Lord did not gift me in that department), to share beauty with the world, or the athletic talent to inspire others through your discipline and dedication.

Every single one of these talents, whether seen on a stage or in a quiet moment, is designed for His glory. And yet, in all of this, we so often find ourselves thinking we know better than the God who created us. I've noticed how, in our humanity, we tend to get in our own way. We can become so confident in our own intelligence, in our abilities, that we begin to think we know more than the living God. We think we've got it all figured out, but we really don't (kind of like the teenagers we parent). We seem to forget our smallness in this vast world. Job's friends spent chapter after chapter debating why Job was enduring such pain. They offered their thoughts and theories, they gave well-intentioned advice—but they didn't know. Really the only good thing they did was sit with him in silence those first few days.

I think that most of us, when we see someone in pain, want to try to fix the situation. We want to make them feel better. We want to explain everything away or wrap it all up with a pretty bow, but sometimes life really takes the wind out of us. And sometimes we just have to sit in that for a bit. Just validate their pain. "Yeah, friend, this sucks. I hate this for you. I wish I could take it away and make it better, but I can't, so I will sit with you in it and I will walk with you through it. Whatever that looks like. I'm here for you. You don't have to do this alone."

Thirty-eight chapters into the story, the Lord finally spoke. I imagine the storm swirling as God's voice echoed through the chaos. Can you picture it? The Creator of the universe, the One who holds the stars in place and knows them by name, began to speak—and not with comforting reassurances but with questions that cut right through Job's finiteness.

> "Who is this that darkens counsel by words without
> knowledge?
> Dress for action like a man;
> I will question you, and you make it known to me.
> Where were you when I laid the foundation of the earth?
> Tell me, if you have understanding." (Job 38:2–4)

God doesn't offer answers here. He challenges us deeply. For the next three chapters, He questions Job relentlessly, asking him where he was when the oceans were formed, when the morning stars sang. He asks Job if he's ever commanded the dawn, if he understands the vastness of the earth, if he knows the source of light and darkness.

With each question we begin to see the illusion of our human power in these situations fading away, revealing the majesty and sovereignty of God. God was reminding Job—and you and me—that His knowledge is beyond our comprehension. He governs not just the light but also the darkness, not just joy but also sorrow. Every drop of rain, every flash of lightning, every moment of suffering is woven into His loving, divine plan.

> "Have you entered into the springs of the sea,
> or walked in the recesses of the deep?
> Have the gates of death been revealed to you,
> or have you seen the gates of deep darkness?"
> (Job 38:16–17)

Granger and I travel a lot for work, and each time we fly, as we take off and ascend high above the people and cars and buildings below, I look out the window and am reminded of just how infinitely small we are. And peeking through that airplane window is just a tiny glimpse of the earth below. How small we truly are in comparison to the One who formed the universe. And yet we in our pride dare to question Him because we think we could do it better. But Job's response says it all. After hearing God speak, Job didn't try to justify himself. He didn't argue. He said rightly, "I am of small account; what shall I answer you? I lay my hand on my mouth" (Job 40:4).

That's the place where we all need to come—to realize our smallness before the Almighty. Who are we to question the ways of God? His wisdom far surpasses ours. It's almost laughable when we compare our fleeting, limited understanding to His infinite wisdom.

So Job repented of speaking presumptuously about God's ways. While he never cursed God, Job did express confusion, did struggle with frustration, and did seem to demand explanations, questioning God's governance of the world.

> "I know that you can do all things,
>> and that no purpose of yours can be thwarted.
> 'Who is this that hides counsel without knowledge?'
> Therefore I have uttered what I did not understand,
>> things too wonderful for me, which I did not know.
> 'Hear, and I will speak;
>> I will question you, and you make it known to me.'
> I had heard of you by the hearing of the ear,
>> but now my eye sees you;
> therefore I despise myself,
>> and repent in dust and ashes."
>> (Job 42:2–6)

We can, and should, take our questions to God. In fact, He invites us to come to Him with our doubts, our pain, and our burdens. Throughout Scripture, we see His people crying out to Him in their distress, pouring out their hearts in raw, honest lament—just like we find in the Psalms. Life can be so overwhelming, filled with moments that break our hearts and leave us feeling lost, confused, and on the bathroom floor. And it's okay to not have all the answers, to not understand why things happen the way they do.

When we bring our questions to God, we must do so with humility.

But when we bring our questions to God, we must do so with humility. We can ask why, but let's remember that He sees the full story, while we see only a fragment. He knows the beginning and the end, and

His ways are higher than ours. Trust that while you may not see the full picture right now, every piece of the story He's weaving is part of something far greater than we can imagine.

We shared this poem at River's service, and it's a wonderful reminder of the divine workings of a God we cannot see.

THE WEAVER

My life is but a weaving
Between my God and me.
I cannot choose the colors
He weaveth steadily.

Ofttimes He weaveth sorrow,
And I in foolish pride
Forget He sees the upper,
And I the underside.

Not till the loom is silent
And the shuttles cease to fly,
Will God unroll the canvas
And reveal the reason why.

The dark threads are as needful
In the weaver's skillful hand
As the threads of gold and silver
In the pattern He has planned.

He knows, He loves, He cares;
Nothing this truth can dim.
He gives the very best to those
Who leave the choice to Him.[1]

In the last chapter of Job, after all the questions and all the suffering, we see that the Lord was not angry with Job for voicing his pains. His anger was directed at Job's friends:

After the Lord had spoken these words to Job, the Lord said to Eliphaz the Temanite:

> "My anger burns against you and against your two
> friends, for you have not spoken of me what is right,
> as my servant Job has. Now therefore take seven bulls
> and seven rams and go to my servant Job and offer
> up a burnt offering for yourselves. And my servant
> Job shall pray for you, for I will accept his prayer not
> to deal with you according to your folly. For you have
> not spoken of me what is right, as my servant Job has."
> (Job 42:7–8)

After Job prayed, something incredible happened. God restored him. (Prayers matter, friends!) Scripture says that *the Lord* gave Job twice as much as he had before. It's not just that Job's possessions were restored; his community returned to him. His brothers, sisters, and all those who had known him came to comfort him. And I think it's so telling what the Bible tells us they comforted him for: "For all the evil that the Lord had brought upon him" (Job 42:11).

That's right. Scripture says the Lord brought this adversity upon Job. It doesn't say Satan alone, or man. It says the Lord. And yet the end of Job's story is not one of suffering but of blessing. "And the Lord blessed the latter days of Job more than his beginning" (Job 42:12).

We don't always get to see the why behind our suffering, and we won't always be restored as Job was this side of heaven. Some may suffer all the days of their earthly lives. Some may never see the blessing after the pain, but I urge you to run to the Scriptures when your heart and your flesh fail. Run to the Scriptures when the Enemy or those around you tempt you to curse God. When feelings lie, run to the Lord for truth.

While we may never know our why for the adversity we face, the Bible gives us several reasons for the pain we endure. Sometimes we suffer simply because we live in a fallen world. Other times our suffering is a direct result of our own sin or the sin of others. And finally, we have a real enemy who prowls around, seeking to steal, kill, and destroy (John 10:10). But ultimately, everything—everything—that happens in our lives is either ordained or allowed by our sovereign God, for purposes that are beyond our understanding. When we come to this realization and we are able to shift our perspective of suffering in our hearts and minds, things change. Our prayers change. Our trust changes. We become rooted in the truth. We must have a right view of God, or we will have a wrong view of everything else.

There is no comfort in the idea that God is distant or removed from our trials. If someone tells you, "God had nothing to do with your suffering," then where does that leave you? Where was He in the moment of your deepest pain? That's an even more terrifying thought.

I believe the Scriptures show us a faithful and reigning God who is present in every trial and every moment of suffering. He hasn't stepped away or lost control; He's right where He's always been—ruling with perfect authority, fully aware of what each of us needs to be shaped more like Christ. It's easy to want to place blame on man or Satan for every trial, but when we do that, we're putting the power in the wrong place. We lose the comfort of knowing that nothing happens outside of God's control.

Now, that doesn't mean God delights in evil and tragedy—He's not the one pulling the trigger in a shooting or forcing someone to get behind the wheel intoxicated. We are still accountable for our sin and rebellion. These are hard truths to hold together, and sometimes it's difficult to grasp how God's sovereignty and man's responsibility can both be true and run parallel at the same time. But the beauty of God's power and rule is that even in the midst of human failure, pain, and evil, He holds it all and is working it all together for His greater plan.

We are not God. His wisdom humbles us, and rightly so. As 1 Corinthians reminds us, "Let no one deceive himself. If anyone among you thinks that he is wise in this age, let him become a fool that he may become wise. For the wisdom of this world is folly with God" (3:18–19).

Oh, that we would all respond like Job, falling on our faces before the Lord, admitting our smallness in the face of His magnificence: "I will proceed no further." That's the cry of true surrender. An acknowledgment that God alone is God, and we are here to trust and to follow, no matter the cost this side of glory.

So, the next time someone asks you, "Where is your God in all of this suffering?" you can answer with confidence: "My God is exactly where He has always been—on the throne. Ruling, reigning, transforming, and redeeming, He is working this for my good and His glory, and I will trust even when I can't see. Because He's right here with me on the bathroom floor." And sometimes in the midst of our darkest moments, God sends His light, reminders of His presence. For me, that light came through an unimaginable connection that only God could have orchestrated.

Eighteen
THE RECIPIENT

And we know that for those who love God all
things work together for good, for those who are
called according to his purpose.

Romans 8:28

The process of organ donation is incredibly private. There's a waiting
period before you can even try to reach out to the recipients. I knew
from the moment we made the decision that I wanted to meet whoever
would receive River's organs. I knew a piece of him would still be out
there, bringing life to someone else.

The process starts with a letter. You write it, pouring your heart
into it, and turn it over to the donation organization. Then you wait.
If the recipient chooses, they can accept and agree to share their contact information, and from there, you can connect if both sides are
willing.

When a letter arrived in the mail telling me who River's organs had gone to, I was shocked. I had always pictured them going to children. River was so small, just three years old. But instead, River's gift went to a forty-nine-year-old woman and a fifty-three-year-old man. I sat with that for a while, trying to understand it. But as with so much of this journey, God's plans are often so different from what we imagine.

I wrote them each letters telling them all about our sweet boy. His beautiful red hair, his deep brown eyes, the way his face would light up when he saw a dinosaur or a tractor. How he loved being outside, digging in the dirt, how he was so full of joy and life. I told them about the difficult decision we made and how we prayed over it. I told them I was praying for them now and that I hoped they were joyful and healthy and thriving. I left the door open, letting them know I would love to meet them someday if they ever felt ready.

Four months after River passed, I received a card in the mail. It was from the recipient of River's right kidney. The simple card read:

My name is Elda. I am 49 years old, married, and have one son. Since I was 14, I have suffered from a painful illness called polycystic kidney disease. Now, thanks to you, I have a second chance at life. Words cannot describe how thankful I am. My family and I will be forever in your debt. I am truly grateful for the new life you and your family have given me. I wish you and your family a long and prosperous life. Sincerely, Elda.

I sat in my car after reading it, and the tears just came. So many emotions hit me at once. Sadness, yes, maybe even a little selfish sadness. I don't know what I had been expecting, but somehow, I wanted more. I craved a deeper connection, something that would ease the ache in my heart. But as I sat there, I realized how much it must have taken for Elda to write those words. I was so grateful that she had even responded and even more grateful that River had been able to give her this second chance.

We finally met on November 11, 2022. I chose a local coffee shop, and we found a quiet table in the back. Maverick, who was just over a year old at the time, came with me. Elda brought her sister to help translate, as she mostly spoke Spanish. She was absolutely precious, standing just over four feet tall with short, highlighted brown hair and warm brown eyes behind her glasses. She wore a lovely floral paisley top with black pants and a cozy black sweater. As we sipped our drinks, she shared her story, how she had been on dialysis for three long years before receiving River's kidney, tethered to a machine for eight to ten hours every single day.

Three years. For River's entire lifetime she had been fighting this battle, hooked to a machine, waiting, praying, hoping, longing for healing. It struck me how we don't always see what the Lord is doing. How often must she have wondered, *Do you see me, Lord? Why are You allowing me to suffer like this?* And yet, in His kindness, I can almost hear Him whispering, "Hold on, child. I am preparing something for you. I'm raising up a little boy who will help heal you. Just hold on."

I have a picture of her holding Maverick that day at the table, and it makes me emotional every time I look at it. It's the closest Maverick has ever been to a piece of his big brother. Elda and Maverick—two blessings that came out of the breaking of my heart. Two lives I will cherish forever.

Elda and I have stayed in touch since then. She recently sent me a picture from a trip she took to the beach in California with her husband. They're both standing there, beaming, with the vast, blue ocean waves crashing behind them. Elda is proudly wearing a red Live Like Riv T-shirt. My heart nearly burst when I saw it. It was a moment of pure joy, a glimpse of God's goodness woven into all the pain.

Even when we can't see what He's doing, even when the path

seems dark and full of heartache, God is always working for our good. Sometimes it takes years to understand it, and sometimes we never fully do, but His goodness never fails.

Even when the path seems dark and full of heartache, God is always working for our good.

When we think of our deepest pain, it's natural to focus on what we've lost or what's been damaged. In those moments, it feels like the world is closing in, and it's easy to believe that our suffering is solely about us. But what if it's not? What if God is using that very pain to set the stage for blessings that stretch far beyond our own lives?

Take Scott Harrison's story, for example. He was living what most would call a "dream life" in New York City—a successful nightclub promoter surrounded by wealth and excitement—but inside, he was dying. He was lost in alcohol and drugs and wealth that left him spiritually empty. In his lowest place, he thought about what his life would look like if he did a complete one-eighty. So he aimed to serve the poor and needy for a year. He made a radical decision to serve people in Liberia, and what he saw on that journey changed his life. People were suffering from diseases that stemmed from one simple thing: lack of clean water.

Scott witnessed children drinking from mud pits and contaminated streams. Women would walk eight hours to fill one jug of water that equaled two toilet flushes for us here in the States. Moved to action, he founded charity: water, a nonprofit dedicated to bringing clean water to people around the world. Something as basic as water—something we waste without thinking—became the life source that could transform entire communities.

Here's where the thread of my own story is woven into his. After River passed, I was driving in Dallas and heard on the radio about Scott and the organization charity: water, and I just knew in that moment we had to give from the River Kelly Fund. By the kind donations of those who cared about River and our story, we were able to fund an entire clean water project in Malawi, providing access to something we often take for granted. This wasn't just a donation; it was a gift born out of our grief. Through the loss of our son, and amazing donors over the past five years, we've been able to give to over thirty nonprofits across the globe almost half a million dollars, and this particular gift—the gift of clean water—moved me to tears.

You see, our suffering isn't just about us. In God's grand design, He is weaving our lives together in ways we may never fully understand this side of heaven. When we're in the middle of our pain, it's hard to see how God could use it for good. But He does.

God is always moving, even in our brokenness. He takes the shattered pieces of our lives and uses them to bring healing, not just to us but to others we may never meet. Our suffering, in His hands, becomes part of a much larger story—one that's filled with hope, redemption, and the unexpected blessing of seeing how He works through us to bless others.

We often receive emails and messages from people who say things like "Because of your story I've found my faith again" or "Because of River, and seeing how you trusted God in the midst of your pain, I've been able to open my Bible and start healing from my own hurt." These words always move me deeply, but I know that all of it is truly the work of the Lord.

It wasn't River who brought these people back to God's Word. It wasn't me, and it wasn't Granger. As Jesus said in John 6:44, "No one can come to me unless the Father who sent me draws him. And I will raise him up on the last day." Our story, and the way we walked through our painful season, was simply a vessel—a conduit the Lord used to draw people back to Himself.

I am so grateful when people tell me they are beginning to seek the Lord again after witnessing the hope we held on to. Many ask, "How can good come from something like this? How can good come from my baby dying? How can good come from this suicide? How can good come from adultery or from the cancer ravaging the body of someone I love?" These are questions filled with real pain, and they are the same questions I asked when we lost Riv.

But if my pain—if the Lord appointing River to only three short years on this earth—and people witnessing how we walked through that grief helps someone open their Bible again, then that is good. If it helps even one person come to the feet of Jesus, then it's a testament that God can bring beauty out of the deepest sorrow.

Through our tears and heartache, we have seen how God uses the broken pieces of our lives to reflect His love and bring others closer to Him. And that gives me hope. It reminds me that our suffering is never in vain—it can be used for His glory to bring light into the darkest of places.

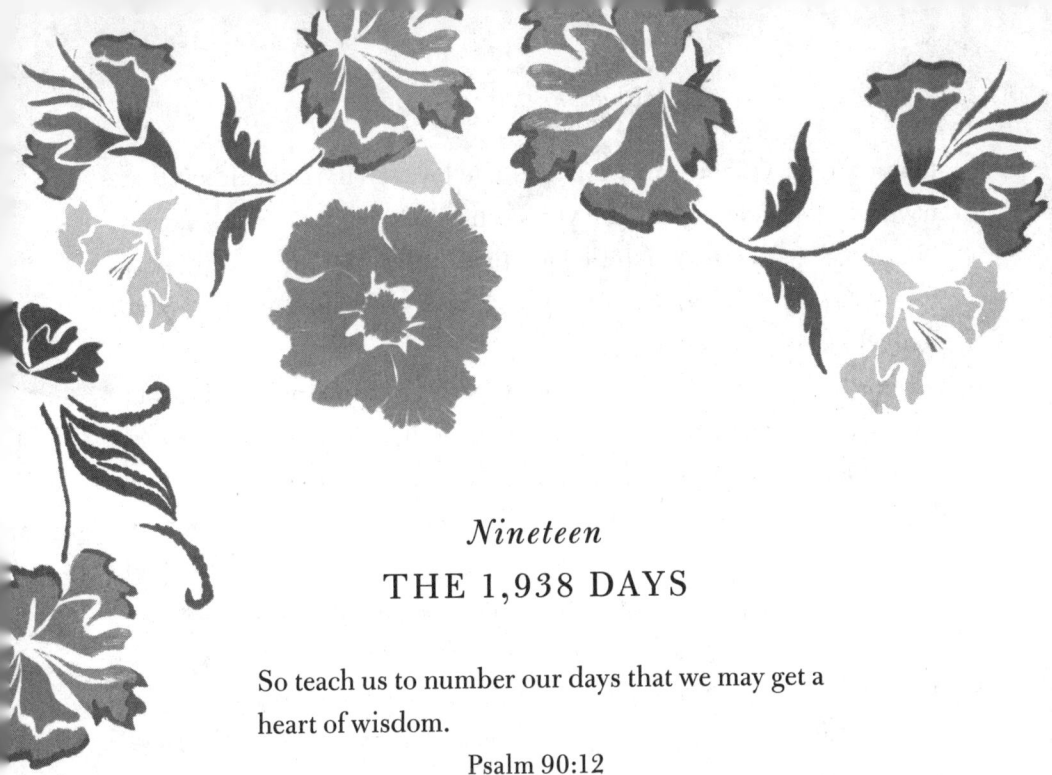

Nineteen

THE 1,938 DAYS

So teach us to number our days that we may get a
heart of wisdom.

Psalm 90:12

As I sit here and write this, it's been five years—1,938 days—since I last
held my lifeless boy in my arms. I've now lived longer without River
than I had him with me here on earth. Even now, it sometimes feels like
a dream that we ever had him—a beautiful, messy, playful, wonderful
dream. Our sweet Maverick has outgrown the age his older brother
ever reached on this side of heaven. These are the kinds of milestones
we've had to navigate along this strange and painful walk through
grief. In certain moments, like when the light hits just right or from
the right distance, Maverick takes my breath away with how much he
resembles Riv. But now, instead of being crushed by the reminder, I
can see it and smile—thanking God for those sweet similarities. Up to
this point we've been able to see small glimpses of his big brother Riv

205

in him. In the way he walks and talks and loves all the same things that have wheels and go fast. And, yes, even in how he, too, is now saying "butthole" with the same inflection that his big brother did. But now we will look to Maverick to see little glimpses of what River may have looked like or enjoyed.

It's been a little over a year since Granger gave up touring. He sold the buses and said goodbye to the fans on his farewell *Like a River* tour. The road wasn't the same anymore, and through Granger's new life in Christ, God changed the desires of his heart and gave him an even more important message to share. He enrolled in seminary and will graduate, Lord willing, in 2027. He's taken mission trips around the world to bring people aid and share the good news of the gospel. I've asked him from time to time if he misses the road life, and he quickly says no. He's found a Treasure, and there is no looking back.

He and I now travel the country giving messages on the hope we have in Christ and coming alongside those suffering, reminding them there is hope and purpose in their pain. We are honored to serve our local church where Granger is now a pastor and serves alongside five other men, entrusted with the privilege of shepherding our local body. Our church is small but thriving, and we are so grateful to be part of a body of believers who love and care for one another deeply. I can't express enough how important it is to get yourself into a local church that guards and proclaims the truths of Scripture.

I've learned so much through all this—about life, marriage, parenting, loss, and most of all, about Jesus. I used to think that with each passing day, I was drifting farther and farther away from River. But now I know the truth. By faith in Christ, I am not drifting away from River at all; I am five years closer to seeing him again. I have more time with him ahead of me than I ever did behind me. And even more importantly, I am five years closer to meeting my Savior face-to-face, this Savior who died for me, who gave His life so that I could be free, forgiven, and adopted. I'm five years closer to falling into His arms and thanking Him for the greatest gift of all—the gift of Himself.

I prayed for the miracle of healing for my son, and I used to say we didn't receive our miracle. But I've realized the miracle wasn't in the healing. The miracle was in the gift of Jesus.

I've come to know that while River was an incredible gift, Jesus is my supreme prize. River is a precious bonus to the ultimate gift of knowing Christ, and my worst day was River's best.

I never would have written this story, this pain, for my life, but God, the author of it all, is writing an even more beautiful story than I could have ever imagined. As I reflect on these past five years, I am reminded of a very simple truth that has anchored me: Life is hard, but God is good. In this world, we will face battles. We will find ourselves on the bathroom floor time and time again because of the fallen nature of this place. But I've learned that with our eyes fixed on the Healer, we are able to wipe our tears a little sooner, and we find the strength to arise a little faster.

I've been on that bathroom floor more times than I care to count. Recently, I was there again with London as she cried over the pain of middle school friends and girl drama. I was there when I learned that a dear friend's husband had passed from his battle with cancer. I wept partly because they were instrumental in my own journey of faith. Their books helped to prepare me for my own season of loss. They showed me how to suffer well, and I wept out of sadness for their family but also out of joy that he got to meet his Maker and he is now whole and healed in the arms of Jesus. And yet again, one Sunday morning at church recently, I found another sister literally lying on the bathroom floor, silently weeping behind a short wall in the corner. People were outside the doors laughing, chatting, some even coming in and out of the bathroom, washing their hands—completely unaware of her. I wondered, *How many had walked past her? Did they not see her, or did they not know what to say if they had?*

But I saw her. The Lord saw her. And just as He has comforted me so many times in my own pain, He led London and me in at that very moment to kneel beside her and offer comfort. It was a sacred reminder that no matter how alone we feel in our grief, God never leaves us. God sees us. He meets us there, on the bathroom floor, in the depths of our sorrow and in the broken places where words fall short. And in His kindness He brings others along to remind us that we are never alone.

I wish I could tell you that when you come to saving faith in Christ, you won't hurt anymore. I wish I could say that life gets easier. But I can't. Until Jesus calls us home, there will be tears. There will be pain. But there will also be His presence, His comfort, and His unfailing goodness that walks with us through every storm. And one day, I can tell you, all the pain will give way to the joy of eternity—with our Savior.

Jesus Himself will wipe away every tear, and sin and death will be no more. Oh, what a glorious day that will be! Hold on, sister. Hold on, brother. Just a little longer. Seek His face, run that race, fight that good fight, and trust in Him with all you have, even if you are crawling into the gates of heaven—because for those in Christ who endure to the end, when you get there, you will hear these precious words:

"Well done, good and faithful servant. Enter into the joy of your Master" (Matthew 25:23).

WATER SAFETY: A LIFESAVING CONVERSATION

I know some may question why, if I believe in the sovereignty of God, I advocate so strongly for water safety. My answer is simple: Trusting in God's plan doesn't mean we live carelessly or ignore opportunities to protect and help others. Just as a firefighter runs into a burning building or a doctor provides care, knowing God is in control, we, too, take action where we can. This isn't a contradiction of faith—it's an expression of it.

We've learned so much about drowning since River's passing. We've learned drowning is quick and silent. It can happen in less than thirty seconds. We've learned it's the leading cause of death for children ages one to four and most often occurs in white males around the age of three—children like River. These facts aren't just statistics; they're a reality that too many families, including mine, have lived through and that isn't discussed enough.

Sixty-nine percent of drowning deaths in children under five happen when they aren't even expected to be near water, during "non-swim times"—bathtubs, toilets, buckets, ponds, pools, oceans, streams, and lakes are all potential risks. Drowning isn't typically the splashing and shouting we see in movies. It's silent and happens within seconds.

So what can we do? How can we take precautions? Water safety requires layers of protection. Relying on just one measure, like supervision or pool fences, isn't enough. Here are some critical steps that can protect the ones we love:

1. Supervision: Designate a "Water Guardian" who watches the water with undivided attention, switching every fifteen minutes. Avoid distractions like phones or retrieving towels.
2. Barriers: Ensure pools have an enclosed fence, at least four feet tall, with a lock, and remove climbable objects nearby. Install locks and alarms on any doors or gates leading to the pool area. Pool covers and nets are a great investment as well.
3. Preparedness: Learn CPR and update your skills regularly. If a child goes missing, check the water first and fast.
4. Bright clothing: Dress children in bright colors to enhance visibility in water.
5. ISR lessons: Enroll children as young as six months in Infant Swim Resource (ISR) lessons to teach them lifesaving skills like floating and self-rescue.
6. Life jackets: Wear life jackets on open water—boats, lakes, rivers, the ocean.
7. No puddle jumpers and floaties: Say no to floaties. These give children a false sense of security in the water. They create a muscle memory that makes children think they can swim and float, but really the floats put them in the vertical drowning position.
8. Swimmer to nonswimmer ratio: Opt for a splash pad or sprinkler if outnumbered by unskilled swimmers. Always

make sure you are holding your child in the water if they cannot swim.

When our son Maverick turned eight months old, we enrolled him in ISR. Tears were shed on both sides. Watching him tumble into the water, rotate his body, and float to find air was both heart-wrenching and empowering. It was something I wish we had known about for River. It's incredible to see what your child is capable of. Mav has since completed lessons at twenty months and at two years, and we just finished his set of maintenance lessons this summer. He can now jump in, float, and swim to the side of the pool.

Whether you have children or grandchildren, babysit children, or simply live in a community with water nearby, this information is for you. Please hear me. Please know this can happen to anyone. Drowning happens to good, loving parents and caregivers.

I pray that by sharing this information we can equip others with knowledge we didn't have. Let's be vigilant, informed, and proactive. God is sovereign, but He also calls us to be His hands and feet—to act in love and protection for those entrusted to us.

For more resources, visit:

- National Drowning Prevention Alliance (www.ndpa.org)
- Levi's Legacy (www.thelevilegacy.org)
- Infant Swimming Resource (www.infantswim.com)

ACKNOWLEDGMENTS

Finishing my first book feels completely surreal—something I never imagined in my own plans. But God had a different path in mind. I'm so grateful for the many people in my life who encouraged and spurred me on every step of the way.

When we were in the depths of darkness, there were so many who cared for us. Too many to recount in this short section. Please know if you cared for our family in any way, provided a meal, sent a card, or even just simply prayed for us, it mattered. We truly felt it all, and your kindness sustained us along this hard road.

Sweet River, though you reached heaven's gate before us, I thank God that you were ours. Without your blessing of a life, this story wouldn't be.

Lisa-Jo Baker: You were my cheerleader from before day one. I am so grateful for your excitement, your encouragement in championing this book to come to life, your tenderness in holding space for our story, your utmost care not only for me but for the reader, and your grace in extending my deadlines more than once when I asked. Thank you for helping me to craft a story that is raw, real, and hopeful, giving God the glory and shining a light for others in pain.

Esther Fedorkevich: Thank you for giving me a chance when you didn't have to. For your honest critiques in telling me during the process when the writing was good but "not great." For pushing me to dig deeper and pull from the depths. You believed our story needed to be heard from the beginning, and I'm honored you made space for it to be told.

Katelyn Harger: You helped to craft the most incredible proposal. Thank you for your time and energy and for still smiling at me on Zoom when I completely changed direction on you. You really helped me to get this thing off the ground. Thank you.

To my incredible best friends and soldier sisters—Heidi K., Marissa, Naomi, Alex, Amy, Kelly, Allison, Becca, Sammie, Celeste, and Heidi U.—thank you for being my unwavering support system. For the coffee dates, lunch dates, Bible study dates, and for the countless prayers and tears shared with me over the last five and a half years. For stepping in to care for my kids when I was overwhelmed and needed space to write, and for lifting me up when impostor syndrome whispered that I couldn't do it. Your love, encouragement, and the ways you carried us after we lost River will never be forgotten. I am eternally grateful for each of you.

My Jesus Girls and GiG Sisters: Your prayers kept me going. They matter! You all are gifts, and I am so blessed to know you and call you all friends and sisters in Christ. Our blood is thicker because of whose blood it is.

Suzanne: My spiritual mama. Words can't express my love for the woman you are. You have helped me immensely on this walk through grief, and I am eternally grateful. You *are* Jesus with skin on.

Nicole Hughes: You saw another mother in pain and you ran toward her. Your honesty and humor in my ache was a balm to my soul. I'm so thankful for this gift of friendship birthed from broken hearts and two incredible little boys.

My SSS: We've been through just about everything, haven't we? Thank you for over twenty-five years of dear friendship and sisterhood. You always show up, not just for me but for everyone around you. I aim to be more like you in that way. You are a light and treasure to this world, and every memory we've made, joyful and painful, is imprinted on my heart. "You can do it, no matter what."

Thank you to the countless other grieving mothers and fathers we have met along the way. Your stories matter. Your children matter. May God continue to heal your hearts as you trust in Him day by day.

To everyone who has contributed to the River Kelly Fund: You have helped this grieving mama find purpose in her pain. Thank you for every single penny. It is appreciated beyond what you will ever know.

Mom and Dan: Thank you for being a safe place for us to grieve. Thank you for constantly reaching out, texting, calling, supporting us, and checking on us in our pain and during this writing process. Your loving pursuit means the world.

Debbee: Your servant heart is truly unmatched. Thank you for leading us in the way of the Lord, for your wisdom, your tears shared in both joy and sorrow, and your time so generously given. You have shown us what it means to love selflessly, walk faithfully, and trust deeply.

JoAnn Barnett: Thank you for your expertise in ISR, for tenderly walking us through the lessons and giving so much of your time and heart. You helped me through something that was really difficult and you gave Maverick a precious gift—the gift of the skills he needs to survive in the water. Thank you.

Vicki Miller: You, too, helped Mav with his water skills. He loved swimming with you. Thank you for your time and love for him and all the children you work with. He can't wait to swim again with Miss Wicki.

To my *Arise with Amber* family: Thank you for showing up every

Sunday to watch a hurting mother fumble with her words as she walked through heartache and tried to find her way around a Bible. Your presence and prayers through that little computer screen pushed me and cheered me on in my walk more than you will ever know. You are chosen.

To the nurses and doctors at Seton Williamson and Dell Children's: We will never forget the love and care you showed for our son. Thank you for walking with us during the hardest three days of our life. What you do matters. Remember that on the hard days.

To the first responders: Thank you for the work you do. Thank you for trying to bring River back to us. Thank you for all the time you give to help others. I pray for you and the things you have to see and endure each and every day.

Granger, baby . . . you told me from the time your book came out that I needed to write mine. Thank you for nudging me to get my story out there and for the perfect book title. Thank you for leading our family with such strength, wisdom, love, and integrity. For being the man the Lord calls you to be for us. I wouldn't change any part of our story. It's a miracle, and there is no one else I would rather share it with than you.

London, Lincoln, and Maverick: You three had so much patience with me over this writing process. Thank you for putting up with me being a scatterbrain and for understanding when I couldn't do all the things you guys wanted to do because I seemed to always have to write. You are the most incredible, resilient, kind, caring, strong, generous, funny, talented kids, and I am so thankful God chose me to be your mama. Watching you grow is one of the greatest joys of my life. Trust in the Lord always. He is the Way, the Truth, and the Life. I pray you not only know Him but love, adore, and behold Him all your days.

To you, the reader: Thank you for taking the time to journey through the words on these pages. My prayer is that this book challenges your heart, encourages your spirit, and stirs within you a heightened passion to know Jesus. Wherever you are in your story, please know this: You are never alone, you are seen, you are cherished, and you are deeply loved.

My Lord and Savior: Thank You, Jesus, for Your grace, truth, and call to arise off that bathroom floor. Thank You for the strength to walk through the valley and share this story. Thank You for Your sacrifice. Thank You for saving me. I am nothing apart from You, and I will sing Your praises until You call me home. I can't wait to see You face-to-face.

NOTES

CHAPTER 8: THE WAILING AND THE SILENCE

1. "This Is a Move," by Tony Brown, Nate Moore, Tasha Cobbs-Leonard, Brandon Lake, single, Bethel Music, 2018.

CHAPTER 9: THE WHY

1. Elisabeth Elliot, *Suffering Is Never for Nothing* (B&H Books, 2019), 9.
2. Annie Johnson Flint, "What God Hath Promised," in *He Giveth More Grace: One Hundred Poems by Annie Johnson Flint* (Hayden Press, 2019), 2.
3. Flint, "He Giveth More Grace," in *He Giveth More Grace*, 1.
4. Kristi McLelland, *Luke in the Land: Walking with Jesus in His First-Century World* (Lifeway, 2024), 50.
5. John Piper, "God Is Always Doing 10,000 Things in Your Life," Desiring God, January 1, 2013, www.desiringgod.org/articles/god-is-always-doing-10000-things-in-your-life.
6. Becky Thompson, *Hope Unfolding: Grace-Filled Truth for the Momma's Heart* (Waterbrook, 2016), 42–44.

CHAPTER 11: THE IDOL

1. Timothy Keller, *Counterfeit Gods: The Empty Promises of Money, Sex, and Power, and the Only Hope That Matters* (Dutton, 2009).

2. John Calvin, *Institutes of the Christian Religion*, ed. John T. McNeill, trans. Ford Lewis Battles (Westminster John Knox, 1960), 1.11.8.

3. Jonathan Edwards, *The Works of Jonathan Edwards*, vol. 17, *Sermons and Discourses, 1730–1733*, ed. Mark Valeri (Yale University Press, 1999), 437–38.

4. J. Li, D. H. Precht, P. B. Mortensen, and J. Olsen, "Mortality in Parents After Death of a Child in Denmark: A Nationwide Follow-Up Study," *The Lancet* 361 (2003): 363–67.

CHAPTER 12: THE WAR

1. Charles Baudelaire, "The Generous Gambler," in *Paris Spleen* (Paris, 1869).

2. R. C. Sproul, *One Holy Passion: The Consuming Thirst to Know God* (Thomas Nelson, 1987), 38.

3. J. C. Ryle, *Practical Religion* (London, 1878).

CHAPTER 13: THE BEACONS IN THE BREAKING

1. Samuel Rutherford, *Ten Letters to the Bruised and Broken*, Relearn.org, August 30, 2024, https://app.relearn.org/tabs/listen/audiobooks/33534.

2. Charles H. Spurgeon, January 22, Evening, in *Morning and Evening: Daily Readings* (Hendrickson, 2006).

3. Oswald Chambers, "You Are Not Your Own," in *My Utmost for His Highest*, utmost.org/classic/ye-are-not-your-own-classic.

CHAPTER 14: THE RACE

1. John Piper, "A Spectacular and Scary Promise," Desiring God, October 27, 2013, www.desiringgod.org/messages/a-spectacular-and -scary-promise.

2. Piper, "Spectacular and Scary Promise."

3. David Gibson, *The Lord of Psalm 23* (Crossway, 2023), 65.

CHAPTER 16: THE MAVERICK

1. "The Dance," by Garth Brooks, track 10 on *Garth Brooks*, Capitol Records, 1989.

CHAPTER 17: THE OFFENSE

1. The authorship of the poem "The Weaver" is unknown; it is in the public domain.

ABOUT THE AUTHOR

Amber Smith is a Christ follower, wife, and mother of four. In 2019 the Smith family suffered a terrible loss when their three-year-old son, River, drowned. Since then, Amber has been on a mission to share her message of hope through suffering to a lost and broken world. She is a speaker, host of the *Arise with Amber* podcast, and founder of the River Kelly Fund. Her aim is to know Jesus and make Him known. She is passionate about studying Scripture and walking with others through the painful parts of life. Amber has a BA in broadcast communication. She and her husband, Granger Smith, live on a little farm in central Texas with their children, London, Lincoln, and Maverick.

GRANGER SMITH

LIKE A

Finding the Faith
and Strength
to Move Forward
after Loss
and Heartache

RIVER

Like a River, a triumphant story of new life birthed out of
tragedy, will teach readers how to face their failures, confront
their pain, and connect with God—the true source of life.